D0934833

JOHN DENVER

JOHN DENVER

Mother Nature's Son

John Collis

MAINSTREAM
PUBLISHING

EDINBURGH AND LONDON

Copyright © John Collis, 1999
All rights reserved
The moral right of the author has been asserted

First published in Great Britain in 1999 by
MAINSTREAM PUBLISHING COMPANY (EDINBURGH) LTD
7 Albany Street
Edinburgh EH1 3UG

ISBN 1 84018 124 9

A catalogue record for this book is available from the British Library

Typeset in Futurist and AGaramond
Printed and bound in Great Britain by Butler & Tanner Ltd, Frome

Contents

Introduction

In 1994 John Denver, with the help of a friendly 'ghost' in the form of writer Arthur Tobier, published his autobiography *Take Me Home*. Although it is not a comprehensive nor even a chronological account of his life – Denver lived in the future, and was clearly not a solemn diarist – it is more revealing, candid and self-critical than his image might lead one to expect. When I was invited to write this book, therefore, it was immediately apparent to me that there was no point in simply embarking on an objective, third-person, updated variation on Denver's own theme. At the same time, what he and Tobier had recorded was obviously an invaluable 'research tool' for which I am hugely grateful.

My own feelings about John Denver and his music suggested a solution – another, more fruitful path for me to follow. I have always harboured some reservations about his catalogue of music taken as a whole, while at the same time being intrigued by it. However, if I felt strongly unsympathetic towards it – and as an unreconstructed rock 'n' roller perhaps I should – I would, of course, have been unable to contemplate spending a year writing about it. I have always been keenly aware that the only market for a book about John Denver is likely to be among his admirers.

My reaction was a little more complex than total acceptance or rejection (I should perhaps state at this point that all indulgence in the first person singular will cease after this brief introduction). I pay tribute to his considerable strengths in the

7

following pages, and assert an admiration for many of his songs – indeed, I have grown to respect his work as a whole while working on this book, and to enjoy vastly more of it than I expected. But I still feel that as a craftsman he had blind spots and weaknesses, and I feel uncomfortable with the relentless optimism of certain songs, while acknowledging that it may well be precisely what others seek. I suspect, furthermore, that Denver attracted a minority of fundamentalist fans who will hear nothing but praise for their hero, who feel unalloyed worship, and I regret that I cannot in all honesty cater for them.

My interest in Denver, therefore, is directed more to other areas of his life and work. He was an industry phenomenon, the most successful American solo artist of the 1970s. This is not only striking in itself, but it implies that he could forge an unprecedentedly strong bridge between himself, his work and the unknown listener. Even beyond those fundamentalists he inspired a legion of fervent Denverites – this is intriguing, and demands respect.

He was an ecological activist and, I suspect, a pantheist – two attributes that further engage one's sympathy. And he was a complex character who wrote uncomplicated songs – he was clearly often at odds with the sanitised image that the world half-knew, and surely he revelled in this contradiction.

I have therefore taken the opportunity to use the charted facts of Denver's life simply as the scaffolding of the present book. They are, of course, constantly referred to and returned to, but meanwhile I have searched for the opportunity to scuttle off and explore something that his life brings to the surface, and that in turn brings him to life. What is offered, then, in the hope that my interest can be shared, is a subjective exploration of the factors that John Denver's life and death bring to mind, given a structure by the objective facts that are available. You, of course, would chart the course of a different exploration, but I argue that it would probably be a parallel one.

ONE

12 October 1997

As someone who had been twice arrested for drunken driving, John Denver could possibly have been flying illegally when he died. On the first occasion, following his arrest on 21 August 1993, he had plea bargained 'no contest' to a lesser charge. He was given probation, and was ordered to play a benefit concert for an organisation who were trying to combat drink-driving by providing the alternative of a free local taxi service.

A year later he crashed his Porsche into a tree near his home in the mountain resort of Aspen, Colorado. It was the night of the final hearing for his second divorce, from Cassandra. After this second drink-driving episode the jury was split. A date for a new hearing was set, and meantime Denver remained in a legal limbo.

Normally someone in this situation would have had his aviation medical certificate revoked pending the trial, and possession of a valid certificate is necessary for a pilot's licence to remain in force. However, Denver had not voluntarily surrendered the document, and so it could perhaps be assumed that he was flying while pending an appeal, even if one had not been formally lodged. A source at the Federal Aviation Authority explained: 'Short of an emergency revocation, the pilot always has due process to challenge the surrender request and a formal revocation if one comes. In this case, no formal official action followed. He was still legal when he flew and he most likely knew it. So do we.'

However, this begs the question as to why the FAA failed to pursue Denver to surrender his licence. And it is in direct contradiction of a further newspaper report that the FAA had disqualified Denver from holding a certificate in March 1997, having learned that he had violated a previous instruction to abstain from alcohol as a condition of flying.

His legal right to be in the air was also challenged by a spokesman for the National Transportation Safety Board, charged with investigating the fatal accident. This source claimed that he had been deprived of the authority to fly in June 1996, when the required medical certificate was withheld on account of the first drink-driving incident.

This is clearly a murky area but also a very important one, given its bearing on such matters as insurance. And also, of course, on the reputation of the squeaky-clean singer: it may well have been a wife-beating drunk who fell into the ocean, a man not so spotless after all. This is not to speak ill of the dead – just the opposite, in fact. Denver was clearly a far more complex, and therefore interesting, person than the straightforward surface of his music at first suggests.

The plane was an experimental, fibreglass two-seater, a 'Long EZ' built from a kit, and Denver had just taken delivery of it from another pilot. He took off from Monterey Airport at five o'clock in the afternoon, local time, and headed out towards the ocean to practise take-off and landing procedures. He made three attempts to relay his position to the control tower, and his last words were: 'Do you have it now?' At 500 feet, just a hundred yards from the shore, the plane made a popping sound, rose slightly and then fell like a stone. It had been in the air for 27 minutes and, according to one eye witness, 'it just sort of dropped unexpectedly into the ocean'.

This was the second time that Denver had crashed a plane – in April 1989 he had crash-landed in a 1931 biplane at an airport in northern Arizona, and climbed out unhurt. In 1995 he was sued by a flying instructor after allegedly taxiing his plane erratically on the runway of a Wyoming airfield. He was, however, a seasoned flyer – a qualified pilot for more than 20 years at the time of his death, and one who had been entrusted with the controls of F-15 fighters. And among his billionaire toys was a Lear jet.

A week after the fatal accident, investigators reported that Denver had simply run out of fuel. Seemingly, he had forgotten to check the tanks before take-off, tried to switch to the emergency tank when he realised that the main one was empty, and then perhaps discovered that there was no reserve supply just before his death. It is a matter for conjecture as to how an experienced pilot, as Denver undoubtedly was, could make such an elementary error, surely an impossible mistake if the basic pre-flight routine of safety checks had been followed.

Indeed, subsequent reports suggested that, although there were indications that the plane had taken off while low on fuel, this had not caused the crash – the more straightforward explanation that Denver had simply lost control of an unfamiliar aircraft was deemed more likely. San Francisco television station KRON-TV admitted that its story of Denver running out of fuel could have been an over-simplification of a local newspaper report.

However, when the National Transportation Safety Board had completed its investigation into the tragedy, as reported in the *Aspen Times* of 23 June 1998, a design modification was revealed. Blueprints for the plane placed the fuel selector handle, which enables the pilot to switch from one tank to the other, within easy reach between his legs. But the builder of this particular model, Adrian Davis Jr, placed the handle behind the pilot's left shoulder so that the fuel lines did not have to enter the cockpit. Ironically a well-intentioned safety measure had simply created another potential danger.

Denver was aware of it, too. On the day of his death he and an

11

airfield technician had tried to lengthen the handle by clamping a pair of pincers to it, to bring it within reach. But this *ad hoc* measure did not solve the problem, and so it was abandoned. Rather than a handle which was close and easy to use, therefore, Denver would have needed to take his hands off the controls, remove his harness and twist around in his seat to switch from an almost empty tank to a full one. We will never know how he could have toyed with this problem just before he died without thinking to check the fuel situation. Because it does seem that there was no full tank of fuel, either the main supply or on standby. The investigation showed that, with 15 gallons in its tank, the plane under Denver's two-week ownership had made a test flight, travelled down to the Monterey airfield and then taken off on its final brief journey. This would probably have used a little more than 15 gallons, and there was no record of recent refuelling.

A further revelation was that the plane had a 150 horsepower engine, though the design specified 110 to 115 horsepower. Although there is no suggestion that the more powerful engine was unsafe – the designer said that some modified models went as high as 200 horsepower – it would inevitably have used more fuel than the standard design. Add to this a fuel gauge sited outside the natural field of view, and the cause of the tragedy seems clear.

At the time Denver had been staying in his summer home nearby, out on the Monterey Peninsula. His second wife, Cassandra Delaney, lived close by, and so Denver could visit their daughter Jesse Belle, perhaps even hope of reconciliation. On his last night he ate dinner at a regular haunt, Clint Eastwood's Mission Ranch in Carmel. On the following morning, according to the local *Star* newspaper, he played in a five-ball game of golf at the Spyglass Hill Golf Club, overlooking the bay. But as soon as the game was over he headed for the airport, keen to try out his new plane.

In view of the possible conflict between his drinking and his decision to fly that day, it was stressed after the tragedy that no trace of alcohol or any other prohibited drug had been detected in his body. Norman Hicks, the Monterey county sheriff, commented in *Rolling Stone*: 'No one indicated that he had been drinking anything at all. In fact, the people he was playing golf with say that he had declined drinking a beer that day because he didn't want to impair his flying abilities.' So he had taken his responsibility on board to that extent, but it still seems to be a matter of intepretation, not hard fact, as to whether he should have been in the air in the first place.

The *Star* also revealed some details of Denver's last interview with the paper, describing it as 'eerie'. Talking three days before his death, Denver said: 'When my day comes, I want to be lucky and die doing what I love most – flying. What a glorious way to pass on.' On the following day he had a medical check-up, and was pronounced in excellent health.

The paper also quoted from another prophetic interview. 'I've always been concerned that I'm going to run out of life before all my dreams come even close to being fulfilled,' he said. 'I think that to die before your time, and to me dying before you've really lived, is so tragic. I try to live every day as though it's my last. I hope that when I come face to face with death that I'm ready. I want no regets.' This is indeed eerie, a strange preoccupation for a fit, very wealthy and supremely successful man seemingly cruising contentedly through middle age. Alas, the journey was not proving that contented, and the drinking was an obvious demonstration of underlying depression at the twofold collapse of his family life. The landlord of a historic pub in the West End of London reports that, on his last visit to the UK, he would come in on his own, sit quietly and morosely, and drink steadily. He was not looking for company, and did not want to be recognised. He had sorrows, and he was drowning them.

When Denver's death was reported, President Clinton spoke

in tribute of his 'soaring music [that] evoked the grandeur of our landscape and the simple warmth of human love. He was a dedicated champion of the environment, spending many hours on the vital work of protecting natural heritage. And he opened many doors to understanding among nations, through his tours of the Soviet Union, China and Vietnam.' Mary Travers of Peter, Paul and Mary said that 'if he had sung the telephone book you would have felt a sense of joy with it, because he would have sung it joyfully'.

Another intriguing tribute, published in *Billboard* on 25 October in a Chet Flippo piece headed, 'ARTIST, ACTIVIST DENVER LOST TO CRASH', came from Michael Greene, the president of the National Academy of Recorded Arts and Sciences. Greene made an extraordinarily high claim for Denver in catalysing a shift in social attitudes among a whole generation of 'aware' Americans. He said that Denver's 'voice and music helped an entire generation make the transition from the rebellion of the '60s and the '70s to the positive, proactive naturalism of the late '70s and early '80s'.

This is a somewhat conservative view in that it dismissed the conscience-awakening of the 1960s with the negative, dead-end word 'rebellion' – it was, after all, a rebellion that broke down racial barriers in America and helped to make the Vietnam War untenable, to take just two positive examples – but it is a weighty tribute nonetheless.

Newspaper headlines reporting the news of Denver's death called him the 'Cosmic Cowboy', 'The Space Cowboy', or more simply the 'Country Boy'. To *Rolling Stone* he was a 'country-pop star'. He would have revelled in the attempts to pin down his style. In the UK, the *Daily Mail* piece was headed 'A SINGER WHO REACHED FOR THE STARS BUT ALWAYS FELL TO EARTH', summing up not just the manner of his tragic death but the dichotomy between image and reality – a flawed Mr Clean. And the *Guardian* headline pinpointed another of the contrasts apparent in his life and career: 'LOVED BY FANS, LOATHED BY CRITICS'.

Although *Melody Maker*, which in its heyday provided the broadest coverage of pop music among the UK magazines, seemed to think itself too hip to pay tribute to Denver, the somewhat racier *New Musical Express* did publish an obituary two weeks after the crash. It could not remain entirely respectful, of course – it referred to his 'saccharine pop ballads' and captioned the accompanying picture 'Denver: Fondly Remembered Muppet Guest'. However, it also paid tribute to his visits to the USSR and Vietnam, to his Chernobyl benefit, to the founding of his ecology organisation, Windstar, and to the fact that in 1993 he had been awarded the Albert Schweitzer Music Prize, which is 'given to outstanding humanitarians'.

Colin Escott, who along with Martin Hawkins is the world's acknowledged expert on the legendary Memphis record label Sun, has written at length about Denver and once referred to the disparity encapsulated in the *Guardian* headline. 'When you dominate popular music the way John Denver did,' he said, 'no one can call you "lucky" any more. When you're in the charts for a decade and then some, when you sell out concert after concert, when you set a house record at venues like the Universal Amphitheatre . . . then it means you're speaking for – and to – a generation.'

Escott points out that it is inevitable that when this happens 'the self-appointed pundits, critics and taste gurus will hate you', but that this is irrelevant in the face of the artist's ability to touch so many people's lives.

Denver himself expressed the opinion that 'most of the critics who write negatively about me are people working in big cities, on big newspapers or magazines. I come in singing about the mountains, the wilderness, about love and family.' Escott tellingly describes Denver's vision as that of 'America before the fall'. The fall of Adam and Eve, presumably – fig leaves may be involved, but not the leaves on every autumnal tree.

Denver was a political activist who grew up surrounded by the right-wing military establishment. He was a clean-cut guy who could get nasty. And he was certainly not without a sense of humour. Years after his remarkable dominance of the American charts had ended almost as suddenly as it began, he could make the tongue-in-cheek boast: 'I've got five or six songs in every karaoke bar in the world!' Earlier, on the successful TV specials made during his years of fame, his co-stars were invited to insult his trademark appearance with gusto. When he appeared as Pinocchio, with a daft grin slashed across his goofy face, it elicited the comment, 'That's a face only a woodpecker could love.' On another show, his boyhood dreams of being a star were cruelly put down. 'You got good hair, but it just looks stupid.' He was proud of his success, but not precious about it. And no doubt his vast wealth, in itself a direct barometer of his popularity, allowed him to shrug off the snide remarks about his music and appearance, and even to join in with them.

The music business gets a little uncomfortable when it cannot squeeze an artist into a familiar pigeonhole. As the hints to record-shop assistants used to say on the outer sleeve of vinyl albums, 'File under Rock' or 'File under Jazz' – put a label on it, otherwise we can't sell it. And yet John Denver thrived while always resisting categorisation. Certainly his background was in the folk music of West Coast coffee houses and clubs, but his mature work does not identify him as a folk singer. For a start almost all of his material was contemporary, newly minted, usually by himself. And his producer Milt Okun's liking for 'sweetening' the sound with string sections and woodwind took it a long way from traditional roots.

Some of Denver's songs draw on country-and-western sounds, either in the exhilarating singalong freedom of 'Take Me Home, Country Roads' or in the corny hokum of 'Thank God I'm a Country Boy'. But Denver would never own up to being a country singer – indeed, towards the end of his life he confessed that he felt out of touch and out of sympathy with contemporary trends in country music. By the mid-'80s his relationship with his record company, RCA, had deteriorated because he hated their last-ditch attempt to turn him into a country singer – even though he adopted the pose so superbly. He often sang about the countryside, of course, and about natural phenomena, but that is not the same thing.

And he was certainly not a rock singer. He seems to lack any intuitive feel for the rhythmic pulse of rock 'n' roll, although this may have been simply because he was not interested in exploring it. Similarly with the country-rock hybrid, which usually displays an empathy for the blues that is missing in Denver's work. He does not bend a note, nor employ the bluesman's technique in slurring the third or seventh note in the scale to support the feeling of the lyric. He just hits the notes, pure and simple. As for the sometimes-used term 'countrypolitan', it simply seems too ungainly and cumbersome to try and work out whether it fits.

Instead, Denver drew on existing styles, notably country and folk, but guided them towards the pop mainstream. His songs have the structural simplicity of folk music, and often betray a country twang. But their outstanding quality is found in the purity and range of Denver's voice, and it is this that makes him so distinctive.

Objective listeners undoubtedly find some of his songs overly sentimental, even cloying, without the stiffening sense of irony that can usefully counteract sweetness, and they may feel that as a songsmith, a craftsman, he sometimes seemed too easily satisfied with the technical or rhythmic structure of a piece. Reviewing a 1982 concert for the *St Paul Dispatch,* critic Laura Fissinger expressed these reservations tellingly. 'Apparently, his fans don't notice the lack of artistic and emotional counterpoint, but casual listeners find it a nearly insurmountable obstacle . . . Denver's fans get angry when others call him treacly and sentimental, and it's understandable. The world desperately needs to act on the things he sings about. But Denver's writing is so unrelentingly chipper and clichéd that he too frequently becomes a parody of himself, taking all those worthwhile messages into cartoon land with him.'

But what no one can deny is that his voice was a quite remarkable instrument, and what this criticism ignores is the numerous songs that chart the turbulence of his private life. They may not have the depth of observation and the constantly surprising imagery that one associates with, say, a Bob Dylan, but unrelentingly chipper they are not.

Denver's longtime collaborator, his producer Milt Okun, illustrated one technical aspect of his music – both a limitation and, in its way, a positive virtue – in a reminiscence published after Denver's death. 'Some years ago I was in Salzburg, where John did a Christmas special, *The Sound of Christmas*, with Julie Andrews. A young American woman who managed the King Sisters, who were also on the show, said she loved John's music. She wondered why he never did a song in a minor key. I told her that among 150 songs or so, surely some were written in a minor key. I told John about it, and he thought that was strange. Back in LA, I pored through his catalogue, and I couldn't find a bloody song in a minor key. He lived his whole life in a major key.'

When his vocal virtuosity combines at the highest level with a lyric that effectively expresses his passion for the natural world, we can hear what made John Denver unique. This surely reached a peak in 'The Eagle and the Hawk', an extraordinary marriage of vocal pyrotechnics and pantheistic feeling for nature, a synthesis that belongs to him alone.

This 1971 song made its first appearance on Denver's fifth album *Aerie*. It is little more than a fragment, suggesting a spontaneous burst of inspiration that could not be laboured over for fear of losing the moment, just as Coleridge could work no more on 'Kubla Khan' once his head cleared. It is a moment that

Denver describes in *Take Me Home*. After the huge success of 'Take Me Home, Country Roads' he was approached by the producer of an ABC documentary about birds of prey, Robert Rieger, to contribute a song to the soundtrack. Not only was he keen to comply, having been interested in the fact that the eagle has had a symbolic importance to various cultures throughout history, but it also gave him a good excuse to join the crew out in Idaho, where he made himself useful by helping to shift the filming gear around.

Denver encountered the eagle and the hawk on that trip (two birds, though following the *Oxford* definition of a hawk as a 'diurnal bird of prey', to distinguish it from the owls, an eagle *is* a hawk). The golden eagle was one rescued by the ornithologist working on the film, Morley Nelson, and the hawk was a red-tailed juvenile being treated for a broken wing.

When the young hawk was fit enough to be released back into the wild, Denver was given the eagle to hold. He describes how at one moment the eagle's nictitating membrane lifted from its eye, and the bird gazed at him for 20 seconds. He was struck by the power of the bird's gaze, and humbled by the fact that it was only interested in him for such a short time. 'The eagle sparked my idealism,' he says. 'This is the way I'd stay grounded, by being in nature and teaching about it.' Sadly, of course, Denver was never actually able to stay grounded for long, and his attempts to get closer to the sensation of the eagle's flight eventually killed him.

The song starts with an increasingly urgent, restless acoustic-guitar riff over which Denver's voice soars in, as if approaching from some aural horizon. His voice, impossibly high and powerful, is of course the eagle. As he describes his flight he suddenly hits a thermal and rises even higher. The arrangement on the 'rethought' version cut for the *Greatest Hits* album in 1973, scored by Lee Holdridge, is a complex and daring one, adding to the descriptive power of the piece. Aaron Copland might well have approved of it.

19

For Denver, the eagle symbolises 'all that we can be, and not what we are', and so in this way he adds a philosophic twist to the end of the song, an extra dimension to his celebration of two overpowering natural phenomena – the eagle, and the landscape it is soaring above.

I have dwelt on this particular song at length, and out of chronological context, because it seems to be the pivotal demonstration of Denver's unique power as an artist, and it is a power that will survive when the comparative vapidity of much of his material has been forgotten – or forgiven.

In his feeling for landscape, Denver sits firmly in an American artistic tradition. To an English outsider, one of the most striking contrasts in America is that between areas of overwhelming natural beauty and the ugliness of a car-based, consumer economy. The beauty is partly that of scale, of a vastness that natives of most other countries cannot experience – there simply isn't the space. On the other hand, small-town America is not approached through leafy lanes, but through a gathering clutter of used-car lots, gas stations, warehouses, fast-food outlets and a gaudy, metallic forest of advertising signs.

In-between these two extremes, America has tamed and corralled the natural world, refashioned and manicured nature into a Walt Disney substitute. Suburban rivers bubble through picturesque rock formations which have been bulldozed and cemented into place, a woodland area becomes a 'leisure facility' and gardens are regimented, with blades of grass all of equal length. It is a golf-course world, a fairway to heaven.

This prompted Denver to use the word 'wilderness' frequently, for example in espousing the cause of Alaska. His own wilderness in Colorado was a compromised one, simply because people like him sought it out. His best work, though it shows little sign of grappling with this contradiction, is nonetheless a celebration of wilderness, a recognition of its spiritual force, of the paramount importance that it should survive. And what it had to survive was not just the threat from car-lot, shopping-mall America, but from the tame, suburban pastiche of nature as well.

A recognition and exploration of wilderness, not surprisingly, has been a particular theme of the cinematic medium, America's chief contribution to twentieth-century culture along with the blues, jazz and rock 'n' roll. From its very outset, the American cinema industry devised the perfect vehicle to explore the theme of wilderness, and of man's threat to it – the western. In 1956 the use of landscape with a western theme – a landscape that is not only represented in its own right but also as a psychological symbol – reached a peak in John Ford's *The Searchers,* with John Wayne scouring Monument Valley on an odyssey of revenge. And more recent westerns, notably *The Outlaw Josey Wales, Pale Rider* and *Unforgiven,* confirm that Clint Eastwood is the greatest of all film directors when it comes to marshalling landscape to express ideas. In Eastwood's films we sense that no change of scenery or climate happens by accident, but is being employed to make a deliberate point.

And the taming of the wilderness remains a constant subplot throughout the work of both Ford and Eastwood – the state-of-the-art miners in *Pale Rider,* for example, gouging away mountains with pressurised jets of water, changing the landscape for ever and rendering it barren, are the villains, whereas the sympathetic characters are the simple panhandlers, leaving nature as they found it. The most advanced society in the world has paid a price for civilising the environment. Denver, in his own way, works in this tradition, one of respect for the raw force of nature, and of concern for its survival.

After Denver's death, Milt Okun referred to an earlier recognition of this by an unnamed French broadcaster. 'During the summer of '96 I was listening to France Musique, the French classical station, and they were playing this piece "Joy, O Joy" by Henry Purcell. The announcer said the work reminded him of the finest qualities of the English, just like John Denver reminded him of the best qualities of America, its people and landscapes.'

The possibility that Denver had ambitions to develop further as a musician was hinted at by Okun in the *Billboard* obituary piece. He mentioned an unfulfilled appointment with the singer, scheduled for two days after his death, 'to discuss further album projects, including a symphonic work'. This meeting would have followed a telephone conversation on the previous Friday, when Denver had sounded upbeat about his new ideas. He had already performed at three concerts with the Houston Symphony Orchestra, which had planted the idea of a symphony in his mind. Okun also told *Rolling Stone* that there were further plans for an album of cover versions to be called *Songs I Wish I'd Written*. Whatever he had in mind we can assume that Denver did not intend to keep repeating his greatest hits for the rest of his life, nor would he have been happy concentrating solely on his new-found passion for golf. He still had something more to say.

TWO
The Roswell Incident

John Denver, Henry J. Deutschendorf Jr, was born in Roswell, New Mexico, on 31 December 1943, the son of H.J. 'Dutch' Deutschendorf and his wife Erma Louise, whose maiden name was Swope. H.J. Senior enjoyed a distinguished air force career, including breaking the world speed record in a B-58 bomber in 1961. The fascination with planes was, naturally but ultimately fatally, passed on to his son.

Roswell lies in the middle of a dusty nowhere, which is no doubt why the military moved in, 'Dutch' Deutschendorf among them. The Roswell air field, formerly identified as the army air field, is just outside town. Due south-east, to the north of El Paso, is the White Sands missile range. The names of the scattered townships here reflect immigration – Glencoe, Carlsbad – as well as native American settlements. Lee Van Cleef famously introduced himself into the *Dollar* trilogy with the laconic statement: '*This* train stops at Tucumcari.' This is a Comanche word, probably first applied to a nearby mountain, meaning a place for an ambush or a look-out. And due north some 450 miles, in sight of the Rocky Mountains of course, is the city of Denver.

Just after the Deutschendorf family moved on from Roswell, in pursuit of Dutch's next posting, this little town of Roswell became world famous.

So much military metal has been hurled skywards from White

23

Sands that when the so-called 'Roswell incident' began, on 2 July 1947, the knee-jerk official statements were both predictable and plausible – the mysterious wreckage was that of 'an experimental plane', or fragments of a grounded weather balloon. Just eight days earlier a pilot named Kenneth Arnold, on reconnaissance way up north in Washington State, had reported sighting nine crescent-shaped flying craft, and estimated their speed to be far in excess of anything that airplane technology had yet achieved. He also said that they 'flew like a saucer would if you skipped it across water,' thus giving birth both to the phenomenon of unidentified flying objects and to its central image, that of the flying saucer. Ever since then, alien visitors from outer space have usually chosen saucers as their preferred mode of travel.

So what happened at Roswell, birthplace of John Denver? On that night in July, a Mr and Mrs Wilmot spotted a 'glowing object' heading north-west. This was in the direction of the town of Corona, where next morning rancher 'Mac' Brazel – who had heard a strange explosion during the night – found metallic wreckage scattered over the ground. The metal was thin and featherweight but it resisted bending, and it was scored with mysterious hieroglyphic marks.

When Mr Brazel began to talk to local radio stations, the authorities moved in to silence him and to relieve him of his metallic souvenirs. The wreckage was moved to the air base at Fort Worth, Texas, and was officially described as that of a weather balloon.

In the meantime, however, on the day after the Wilmots' sighting, a civil engineer named Barney Barnett reported finding a 'metallic, disc-shaped object' in the desert on the other side of the Rio Grande, west of Roswell. Inside the crashed craft, for such it appeared to be, and on the sand around it, were what looked like the corpses of small, humanoid creatures dressed in grey, one-piece worksuits. Soon afterwards, the air base reputedly ordered four child's coffins from a Roswell undertaker. For years, the story was buried under an official-secrets blanket, and it was only the Freedom of Information Act of 1976 that forced the publication of government papers on the subject.

Even then, officialdom had an answer. The so-called Majestic-12 files relating to Roswell were, it was claimed, forgeries. Nothing untoward had ever taken place, and these papers had not surfaced through the operation of the new Act, but by the actions of a hoaxer. Indeed, the Majestic-12 papers did apparently come to light on a roll of film sent anonymously to a television producer, not as part of a government open-house exercise, and the signature of President Harry Truman on one of them appeared to be a forgery. Either they were an officially sanctioned hoax designed to discredit the new cult of 'ufology', or forgeries perpetrated by believers to strengthen their case. And yet there had been those apparent sightings, by sober, upright citizens. A pragmatist may explain, quite accurately, that 'flying saucers' are almost invariably optical illusions caused by freak climactic and cloud conditions, but alien corpses lying around in the desert are certainly not.

A huge development in the Roswell story took place in 1995. A film-maker named Ray Santilli had purchased the earliest known film footage of Elvis Presley from an elderly American cameraman, who also offered him film of what he claimed to be an autopsy carried out on a Roswell alien. The cameraman asserted that he had been in the US army in 1947, and had been ordered to cover the event in secret. He further said that he had purloined some of the film, and this is what he sold to Santilli. On 5 May 1995 the film was screened to an audience of ufo experts and science journalists in London.

The film shows a creature lying on an autopsy table. It is shorter than most adult humans, with a large, bald head and big black eyes. It has six digits on each hand and foot, had sustained various injuries and could possibly be a pregnant female. The corpse is first examined, and then dissected, and judging by the clock on the wall of the postmortem room the available film consists of extracts from a lengthy process.

Expert opinion was divided as a result of this eerie film show. The footage could have shown one of three events: the examination of a genuine alien corpse, a special-effects spoof, or the examination of a deformed, perhaps radiation-affected, human. It was then offered for sale on video, with a careful disclaimer stating that the film stock dated from 1947 but that this did not mean that the autopsy necessarily did, that medical evidence suggested that the corpse was non-human but that this could not be verified, and that it was believed to relate to the Roswell incident but that this, too, could not be guaranteed. Extracts were used in a Channel 4 documentary in the UK, and were widely shown in the United States.

Of course, even if the film – mysteriously left to gather dust, apparently, for nearly half a century – is a hoax, that does not mean that the entire Roswell incident is likewise a fabrication. Something, it seems, did indeed happen out there in the desert, and 'Dutch' Deutschendorf's former colleagues were ordered to cover it up. John Denver's autobiography makes no reference to the most celebrated case history in ufology, nor even refers to his birthplace by name, though this is not particularly surprising – his geographically dislocated childhood did not lend itself to detailed reminiscence. But whereas most Nowheresvilles remain in obscurity, Roswell has marked two important births – ufology and John Denver.

THREE

Roots in the Rocky Mountains

It is a precious gift to know where your roots are, where you belong. Somewhere that is a lot more than simply where you hang your hat. It might not be your birthplace, which could have played just a transient role in your parental history, and it certainly might not be where you live now – so often this is due to enforced economic choice or some sort of temporary accident. The Irishmen of north London dream not of Camden Town or Kilburn, where they spend their lives, but of the green fields of Galway, Kerry or Kildare, those fields they had to leave behind. To retain a sense of the homeland, the native turf, helps to maintain a peaceful heart amid the more confused pumpings of modern urban life.

Sometimes that sense has to be discovered later, perhaps as a feeling of having arrived 'home' in a place that is unfamiliar. In John Denver's case the discovery was powerfully described in 'Rocky Mountain High', and it took until his 27th year. On his 1994 *Portrait* video he describes the sensation thus: '. . . Coming to Colorado was like coming home for me. I don't know how to explain that I just felt that this was my home, from the first place that I walked on this little piece of land and began to look out and get familiar with these mountains.' He was indeed coming home 'to a place I'd never been before', as he says in the song.

His early life was perforce rootless. This went with his father's job, constantly picking up and moving on. And wherever Dad

27

did hang his flying hat, his environment was that of the American air force, not of the host community.

When American servicemen travel, whether it be within their own country, to Germany or to the flatlands of eastern Britain, they take the pre-formed trappings of Uncle Sam's military, at work and at play, with them. The immediate world outside, the real world, need not impinge on them at all if they don't want it to. The familiar packaged foods, the frozen beer and soft-pack cigarettes, the baseball magazines, even the entertainers, are all flown in to a sealed world within a world. Years ago I interviewed one of my heroes, the soul singer Percy Sledge, on what I assumed was his first visit to the UK. It turned out that he'd been several times before, to play on American military bases. And so, in a sense, on those occasions he hadn't actually left America. He had no more visited the UK than had Elvis Presley, changing planes at Prestwick Airport on his way home from Germany.

So the young Deutschendorf could never find a home in the spiritual sense, out there beyond the four walls of the service house. Where would it be? In his actual New Mexico birthplace, Roswell, of which he had no recollection whatsoever? In Japan, only the vaguest of memories? Arizona? Alabama? Texas? No, Denver had to find a home for himself, as it happens in Colorado, so much so that he took his name from it as well as putting down those belated roots. This enthusiastic adoption informed his songs and shaped his feelings for the natural world.

On his European side, Denver's grandmother was a Mennonite, a Christian denomination that gained this name in 1541, after the Dutch priest Menno Simons (1496–1561). Mennonites were in a direct line of descent from the reformist Anabaptists, risking persecution simply on account of their deviation from the orthodox. In the case of the Mennonites this consisted of agitation for the restoration of a New Testament church based on the evangelical principle that the Bible is the literal truth.

The mainstream church has always accepted a degree of symbolism and metaphor in the Biblical account – indeed, this is largely what gives it a literary richness beyond its specific function as a description of the 'true way'. To the Mennonite, salvation is only possible by being 'born again' in Christ, a principle that stresses the importance of missionary work and conversion of the heathen. In the America of the 1920s this developed into what was to become known as fundamentalism.

One of Menno Simon's contributions was to draw many isolated congregations of similar-thinking Anabaptists together, to give them a common identity. Later, in the 1690s, they survived a major schism when the Mennonite bishop in Switzerland broke away to form the Amish sect. By the eighteenth century, persecution was speeding up the diffusion of the faith through, in particular, Germany, Holland and the United States, and in the middle of the nineteenth century a group was established in Russia. Many soon fled, prompted by the loss of exemption from military service, and moved to America, settling in particular in the mid-west. At this time others from Germany and elsewhere in mainland Europe, along with economic migrants from the Celtic fringe of Great Britain, were also finding their way to America.

The Deutschendorfs' own roots were in Germany, but in the nineteenth century they travelled east to farm on the banks of the River Volga in Russia. As Europe became threatened with conflict yet again, in the inexorable build-up to the First World War, they made for the quieter farmlands of Bessie, Oklahoma, where a number of Germans had already settled. By this time all of Europe was unstable – Russia had been humiliated by Japan in 1904; the dominant European royal house, the Habsburgs, were in conflict with Russia over what was left of the Turkish Empire; and in June 1914 came the flashpoint, when the heir to the Habsburg throne, Archduke Franz Ferdinand, was assassinated by Serbian nationalists. This ranged Austria–

29

Hungary, supported by Germany, against Serbia. Russia supported the latter, and were allied to France, and when Britain declared war on 4 August a central European squabble had become a global war. John Denver's grandfather had made a shrewd decision to emigrate to the calm flatlands of the American mid-west.

It was here that Denver's German grandparents met, but his grandfather's nationality problems came back to haunt him in 1917, when America entered the war on the Allied side. He was no longer a peaceful immigrant, but a German – the enemy. Rather than risk persecution and internment he walked north – literally – into Canada. After the war was over the family returned to live on a rented farm in Corn, Oklahoma, where they raised 11 children, of whom Denver's father Henry John was the second eldest. As the children grew, music-making became an important part of family life.

On his mother Erma's side Denver's ancestry was Catholic, drawn from both Celtic and German stock, and his grandfather Peter sold motorcycles in Tulsa, also in Oklahoma, until his business went under during the Depression. The family name was Swope, and it was his maternal grandmother, Mattie, who gave Denver his first childhood guitar. He was 12 years old, and the instrument was one that his grandmother had played when she was younger, a vintage Gibson.

Henry John joined the army air corps and met Erma in 1942 when he was stationed in Tulsa. Her parents by this time were running a nearby dance-hall, and she worked there as a waitress. Six months later, when Henry John's training period in Tulsa was over and he was about to be sent to Oklahoma City, they suddenly decided to get married. He was moved to Savannah, where their married life began, and then to California. By now, America had joined the Second World War, following the Japanese attack on the American fleet in Pearl Harbor on 7 December 1941, and Henry John applied to be trained as a fighter pilot. In fact he was taken on as a trainee instructor, moved to Santa Ana and hence to Roswell. And so, even as a tiny baby, rootlessness was already in his son's genes.

John Denver's work, notably the 'open air' songs that ran throughout his career, can be approached from a pantheistic point of view. Indeed, this may help to give some depth and resonance to material that otherwise can seem a little too glib to be truly satisfying.

Like so many philosophical and religious concepts, that of pantheism can to a degree be chiselled and pummelled until it means what you want it to mean. To take it literally, from the Greek root, it suggests that God is in everything and everything is in God. But, as the *New Schaff–Herzog Religious Encyclopedia* points out somewhat resignedly: 'It is a necessarily wide concept resisting a final definition.' It is also a very old concept, though it was perhaps not until the eighteenth century that writers and philosophers tried to pin it down and find a place for it among other beliefs.

From the earliest recorded writing, however, pantheistic concepts have been expressed. Heraclitus saw the Godhead as an eternal living fire animating everything. The Stoics identified a harmonic balance between good and evil at the root of creation. Diogenes identified God as air, reasoning that air permeates everything and without it nothing can survive.

Writing in 1705, the philosopher Toland began to bring the concept up to date. He suggested that all matter is endowed with inherent motion, and so there is no need of an external power to create or control it – God is within the universe, not standing outside it either pulling puppet strings or observing in impotent despair. Spinoza put the same idea rather more bluntly – substance, matter, is all that exists, and it is irrelevant whether you want to call it God or nature. The material and the spiritual co-exist and are as one.

Naturally, commenting from a conventional religious perspective, the *New Catholic Encyclopedia* says rather dismissively that pantheism 'can be reduced to a form of atheism in that identification of God with the world denies Him transcendence – a view fundamental to all theism'.

I would say that yes, of course it is a form of atheism, in that this dynamic in which the spiritual and the material combine has no need of a divine chemist or architect, a supreme being. But the encyclopedia swiftly strikes back, triumphantly pointing out that 'many of those identified as pantheists manifest a strong religious commitment to God'. I have to admit that this is undeniably the case, since they include two of the most persuasive of all pantheistic writers, Samuel Taylor Coleridge and William Wordsworth. And, as several of his songs suggest, John Denver as well. He may have been turned away from organised religion in adolescence, put off by a blinkered school teacher, but not to the extent of rejecting God completely. His pantheism has a religious foundation.

To seek a more up-to-date definition of pantheism, I turn with relief to the latest edition of the *Shorter Oxford English Dictionary* (to those unfamiliar with this verbal treasure trove I should point out that the term 'shorter' simply means that it has been boiled down to two massive volumes). Here we read that pantheism is 'the belief or philosophical theory that God and the universe are identical (implying a denial of the personality and transcendence of God); the identification of God with the forces of nature and natural substances'.

This is as close as we can hope to get to a definition that leads me to claim a belief in pantheism, and to identify Denver with it. It suggests that we can sense within landscape and climate, within the machinations of the natural world, a spirituality, a mysterious force, that somehow informs the harmony of the whole – including, presumably, the universe. This power is felt in conventionally beautiful scenes, of course, of sun setting over water, of light bursting across the green hills. It is felt when faced with environments that hint at a greater spiritual mystery, whether it be the awesome Grand Canyon, the myth-steeped Somerset Levels or Denver's beloved Rocky Mountains. And it is felt in the purely destructive forces that push and shove and threaten to upset that innate harmony, without as yet ever quite succeeding – the hurricanes that visit the Caribbean and the southern United States, the floods that lay waste to Bangladesh, the earthquakes that kill thousands in seconds, the pestilences of drought and famine. From outer space, looking down on the world through a deafening silence, this harmony that can survive such disasters, a harmony of tension as well as balance, must be even more apparent.

Many feel no need to call this spiritual force by the name of God, and certainly feel that it denies the existence of a transcendent being. It is not possible, of course, to make such a claim for John Denver, but a sense of pantheistic mystery is undeniably one way into his songs, a mainspring of much of his creative work and of his work for the environment.

He often touched on the subject in interviews. 'My greatest inspiration has always been the out-of-doors,' he once said. 'The out-of-doors was my first and truest best friend. It was the desert in Arizona when I was in grade school. And later on it was the woods around Montgomery, Alabama. Later on it was the wheat fields when I worked on the wheat harvest. It was the forest and the lumber camp that I worked in when I was in college. Nature has always been my best friend. And my songs are full of images from nature.'

FOUR

A Military Childhood

On 16 July 1945 the US successfully tested an atomic bomb in the New Mexico desert, just a mushroom cloud away from Roswell. On 6 August they dropped the bomb on Hiroshima, and three days later on Nagasaki. In between these two cataclysmic and decisive actions, the Soviet Union joined the war against Japan. Emperor Hirohito accepted the inevitable, told his country that it must 'endure the unendurable' and, on 2 September, Japan unconditionally surrendered. The war was now over – on 28 April Mussolini had been taken and shot by Italian partisans, and on 30 April Hitler had committed suicide. Whether or not the awful and lingering destruction caused by the unleashing of the atom bombs on Japanese civilians was strictly necessary in order to end the conflict, it dramatically confirmed the Allied victory.

In 1946 the Americans began a new programme of atomic testing centred on the Bikini Atoll, one of the Marshall Islands far to the west of Hawaii in the Pacific – beyond the International Date Line, in fact, closer to Japan than to the North American mainland. John Denver's father was assigned to the project as a reconnaissance pilot, with the task of monitoring and photographing the devastation caused by the tests. It was inevitably a worrying time for Denver's mother – not only separated from her husband but, by and large, completely out of touch with him. At one time she saw with horror a newspaper report that his plane had crashed, and it named him as a casualty – in fact the plane had indeed gone down, but he survived with comparatively minor injuries.

America was to remain in occupation of Japan until 1950, and early in 1949 the Deutschendorf family moved there as a result of the next posting. John was five, and his brother Ron was born there. When America withdrew from Japan, the family were relocated to Tucson, Arizona, 100 miles south-east of Phoenix and, like Roswell, another desert town. John recalls being something of a loner, but the fact that the town stopped and the desert started just three blocks away from his home gave him an early taste of the power of landscape, and of the companionable strength of unspoilt countryside. Sometimes his father would drive him deeper into the wilderness than he could explore on his pedal bike, up into the mountains to the west of the town.

But John spent more time on his own than with his father, who was a somewhat distant figure, very involved in his work. Late in 1950 America went to war again, this time in Korea. Communist-controlled North Korea invaded the south – one of the countries to have received American financial help since the end of the Second World War, intended as a bulwark against Communism – on 25 June. Though war was not officially declared, once America had weighed in to support South Korea, and China sent troops to aid the north, it was indeed a war in all but name. Inevitably John's father was not only busy, but once again away from home for long periods. His duties included the training of pilots and flying on temporary duties for Strategic Air Command, and his absences could last as long as three months.

John was enrolled in the Tucson Boys' Choir, and he and Ron attended the Presbyterian Church of the Covenant. One experience at the age of 12, which he identifies as causing him to question formal religious teaching, will strike a chord with many people who remember finding a religious upbringing suddenly challenged by the curiosity of youth. One of his classmates asked a question regarding the parable they were studying, and the teacher would not discuss it – religion had to be swallowed whole, as the complete and only truth, and it was not a matter for debate. This age, the immediate pre-teen period, is surely when important questions begin to formulate in one's mind for the first time, and the possibility of discussing issues that had until then been meekly accepted becomes headily apparent. No longer need everything be taken at its face value – this is not the dangerous seed of rebellion, but of intellectual curiosity.

One wonders how many children, of all faiths, have either been put off religion for life or turned away from it for years by such incompetent teaching – a simple failure to recognise that, far from stifling curiosity in favour of meek acceptance, a refusal to discuss an important issue totally undermines its validity. Here is the truth, and it's the truth because I say so. Copy it down in your exercise books, memorise it, repeat it and don't ask questions. Class dismissed.

It was at this point in his life that Denver found himself becoming what he identifies somewhat precociously as a 'social activist', in that he stood up against bullying, seeing the injustice of identifying and exploiting an underdog, and of racial discrimination. He became aware that he could play with a black kid at school, and yet he wouldn't invite him home. This contradiction was to become even more pointed in the town that was to be his father's next posting.

Of this further staging post in his childhood – Montgomery, Alabama – it is striking that in his autobiography Denver identifies the town with a heroine who might not have occurred to everyone, including perhaps his militaristic father. A woman by the name of Rosa Parks, by refusing to go to the back of the bus, became a catalyst and potent symbol for the first stirrings of the black civil rights movement.

The famous incident recalled by Denver had taken place on 1 December 1955, two years before his family moved to Montgomery. Parks, a 43-year-old black woman, climbed aboard a Cleveland Avenue bus and took a seat towards the front. It was not long before a white, male passenger made a point of challenging her, demanding that she give up her seat to him and retreat humbly to her rightful place at the back. She refused, the bus was stopped, and she was arrested.

News of the incident instantly spread across the city. Black women met to demand a boycott of the city's buses, and this strategy was taken up by their community leaders. They decided on 5 December for the boycott demonstration, and elected the pastor of the Dexter Avenue Baptist Church to be in charge of publicising the event, and furthermore to become president of the newly-inaugurated Montgomery Improvement Association. He was, of course, the Reverend Martin Luther King Jr.

Montgomery's black population numbered some 50,000 at the time, and they made up 75 per cent of the city's bus passengers. They responded to the boycott call although, since at this stage the association did not apparently look beyond the protest action and demand immediate desegregation of public transport, the demonstration did not receive the official blessing of the National Association for the Advancement of Colored People. But the boycott went on for a year.

On 13 November 1956 a Supreme Court ruling declared segregation to be unconstitutional, and on 21 December, once the city had formally announced its compliance with the ruling, the boycott was called off. King, who had been arrested and fined $500 for illegally encouraging the boycott, and who had seen his house bombed by racists, made a concise statement of his central belief: 'Non-violence is the most potent technique for oppressed peoples.'

In February 1957 came the formation of the Southern Christian Leadership Conference, an interracial society designed to co-ordinate peaceful protest against discrimination. Dr King was elected its head. And in August of that year the Civil Rights

Act finally won approval in the Senate, after the longest 'filibuster' attempt on record, when the racist Senator Strom Thurmond of South Carolina spoke for 24 hours and 18 minutes to delay the act. Another landmark incident occurred in September, when with the deployment of 1,000 paratroopers and 10,000 National Guardsmen – a graphic illustration of the strength of racist fury against such a move – black children at last entered Little Rock Central High School. This inexorable process had been set in train by Rosa Parks, citizen of Montgomery, and her action had clearly lingered long in the young John Denver's mind.

His family didn't move there until 1957, when his father was posted to the War College at Maxwell Air Force Base, but Denver already knew of it as 'a city of discrimination and hate and the last place I wanted to be'. Maybe, however, being at the eye of the racial storm during this turbulent period also meant that Montgomery showed the way towards a more equitable future. Ironically, the school that Denver went to was still effectively segregated – such a recent law had yet to become practice, just weeks after the violence of Little Rock – whereas in less racially sensitive Tucson the classes had been mixed. And it wasn't just a question of skin colour – the surname 'Deutschendorf' was clearly considered to be more suggestive of apple strudel than Mom's all-American apple pie. In an atmosphere in which classmates could brag of trips to the black ghetto of Montgomery, 'Niggertown', in order to harrass the residents, the young Deutschendorf was always going to feel out of place. And so, as when he lived in Tucson, the surrounding countryside exerted a growing fascination, and he took to swimming and fishing in the nearby lakes. Nature was an escape.

Because John and Ron grew up at the behest of their father's work moves, rather than the school calendar, he entered the ninth grade in Montgomery a week after everyone else in the class, and was therefore an instant outsider. What finally gave him contact with his peers, of course, was his developing skill on

39

the guitar. He had mentioned guitar-playing in a class questionnaire, and so his music teacher persuaded him to bring his instrument into class, to play and sing – the choice included Paul Anka's then-current début hit 'Diana', based on the four-chord sequence that served doo-wop and teen ballads for a decade or more. He recalls that he'd also written a couple of songs himself by then. John established an identity within the school community through his music – as he put it: 'People started saying "hey" to me . . . [they] knew who I was and it really helped me make friends.' But no sooner had he done that – retaining, no doubt, an early taste for public performance – than the family was on the move again.

This time the trek was due west back towards Tucson, across Mississippi and Louisiana some 600 miles into Texas, for a posting at Fort Worth. It was here, as a squadron commander flying B58s, that John's father broke the speed record, and where his combined love of planes and the military life seemed to reach its satisfying peak. Deutschendorf Sr was fulfilled, in the only professional and ethical life he knew.

His elder son settled in more slowly, being neither a natural ball player – a compulsory skill in Texas – nor at ease with his female classmates. But music continued to offer his own route towards establishing an identity. In the summer vacation, as his father had done before him, John worked on the Oklahoma farm of a family friend. Sitting on a tractor under a big sky, with acres of wheat around him, he felt at home and at peace. Less rewarding was an after-school job washing dishes at the McCrory Five and Dime. At school, though, the most satisfying moments remained those when he was relating to his guitar rather than to other people.

As he recalled to Chet Flippo in 1975, when he earned the accolade of a *Rolling Stone* cover feature: 'My activities were centred around school and football and church and senior high fellowship, and I got together with a couple of bands and started

40

playing parties, proms, stuff like that. It was the music that really worked for me. It was the thing that I always did that was easy and made me feel good. I liked singing for people.' When he graduated, he moved on from his grandmother's 1910 Gibson acoustic – his parents bought him a Fender Jazzmaster and Fender Pro Amp.

John acquired a driver's licence as soon as he was old enough, and in-between a summer of farm work and his last high-school year he briefly worked as a truck driver for his uncle Dean. From the tractor to the truck, he was getting to like a steering wheel in his hands almost as much as the guitar, seated in his private world, in control. The ability to drive gave a sense of independence to a young man still painfully gauche at forming relationships with his peers – he tells in passing the story of throwing a party to which nobody came, which must be as lonely and hurtful an experience as a shy adolescent can ever be hammered with. This is surely the sort of emotional bruising that might never heal, that continues to fire off twinges during sleepless nights for ever. Maybe platinum albums were the eventual balm, enabling the mature man to be so seemingly off-hand about such a teenage horror. Soon afterwards his uncle Dean died, ironically in a car crash, his alienation from his father grew, and his parents were arguing. The scene appeared to be set for escape.

The last straw was one Friday night. Having asked a girl out on a date, a rare event in itself, he had to cancel because his father had the old car that he was allowed to use on such occasions. His father was at the officers' mess, drinking with his friends after a week's work, and when he came home drunk he started an argument with John's mother. John left home the next morning before the household was awake, heading for Los Angeles. 'It came out of all the conflicts that happen between parents and their children who can't communicate,' he told *Rolling Stone*. 'Things weren't right and I felt responsible for it and felt that I should just leave. I didn't want to but that's what I did.'

There must have been a road movie running in his head that day – the best part of 1,500 miles, due west to El Paso. He travelled on for a Saturday overnight stop with friends in familiar old Tucson, and then continued towards the coast the following day. He didn't have it in mind to try his luck at music – he vaguely nurtured the romantic Hemingway idea of getting a job on a boat. Then, when he arrived at the coast, he decided on a more practical course – to call the home of friends of his parents; Carl Hart, a civil engineer, and his wife Nina. However, he couldn't find them listed in the phone book. In fact they were in Long Beach, not Los Angeles itself, and so the second night of his expedition was spent sleeping in the car.

Meanwhile, it transpired, his father had been flying over the routes of the main highways, first north and then west, looking out for him. Without anywhere to go – and now the car wouldn't start anyway – John was forced to call home. His father gave him the Harts' telephone number, and set out after him. On the long journey back, the conversation was as stilted as ever, but a blow for freedom had been struck. However, as he observed: 'I don't know that anything was really solved then.'

John now had to decide what to do after high school, and eventually enrolled at Texas Technological Institute in Austin, to study architecture. It was 1961, he was 17 years old, and on the drive south to start his career as an architect his father gave him advice which stayed with John all his life. It seems to illuminate their relationship, as well, in his father's choice of words, which Denver quoted in his book. There is love and respect there, as there should be in any decent family. But there is also a chill about the words, a deliberate distancing, an inability to pay a compliment without immediately qualifying it: '. . . You've got a talent. You can play guitar and you can sing. Not everybody can do that, but that doesn't make you any better than anybody else. Just remember that.'

John regarded his college studies as a bearable irrelevance while he developed his skill and enthusiasm for music, even occasionally getting paid for performing with a college group called the Alpine Trio. There was also the thrill of adolescent freedom. 'All of a sudden I was on my own, didn't have to go to bed at any particular time, could study when I wanted to . . .' By his second year, he told *Rolling Stone*, 'I was playing with a band again . . . a lot more than I ever had before and I was also singing by myself.'

Prophetically, he cites those he listened to in particular as Joan Baez, Tom Paxton, the Chad Mitchell Trio, Peter, Paul and Mary and the New Christy Minstrels. Or maybe the list was tidied up with hindsight to those who were to be central to his career. 'That was the kind of music I had been singing and now it had a label. People called it folk music.'

By his third autumn at Texas Tech, the time that American history was forever changed by the assassination of the President in Dallas, just next door to Fort Worth, it was clear that music had won out over architecture. By this time, November 1963, his father had moved on yet again, and the family home was now down in Florida. After Christmas there and a further month of the New Year failing to buckle down to his studies, John gave up architecture, faced up apprehensively to the inevitable parental disapproval, and made another stab at Los Angeles. His father contributed a grudging and no doubt worried $250, while the Harts – now that John had their address and telephone number – were once more a point to aim at.

'Everybody – and I mean everybody – said that I was making the biggest mistake of my life. Also I found out they'd been betting on how long I was gonna last . . . my friends in the architecture department . . .' As for his parents, he summarised their opinion as: 'We don't approve of this, we would prefer that you stay in college and we think you're gonna slouch around and when you get tired of playing around like that, then let us know, and we'll help you on from there with your education.'

43

FIVE Into the Clubs

Whatever era and whatever style is involved, popular music has always needed an open door through which young hopefuls can walk, with the intention of making a name for themselves. This is how the music is nurtured from the roots upwards, for without it we could only be left with the pop Svengalis who manufacture a commercial sound and then go looking for puppets to perform it to their specifications.

So folk clubs have a floor spot, open to members of the audience. On a quiet night bars and pubs will put on unknowns, maybe on the basis of a half-decent demo tape. Elvis Presley started in a similar way, walking into the Sun studio in Memphis not to audition, but simply to make a one-off acetate as a present for his mother. Luckily for him and rock 'n' roll history the studio secretary Marion Keisker heard him, and pestered boss Sam Phillips to send for the young truck driver. The ambitious young Frank Sinatra invested in sheet-music arrangements and persuaded band leaders to allow him to fill in during the interval. So it was with John Denver – and the floor-spot singer was soon to be heard by influential ears.

He arrived in Los Angeles in 1964, and as he drove down Sunset Boulevard he spotted the RCA building and claims to have dreamed of recording there, making the association in particular with Elvis Presley and Paul Anka. He paid his way at first by working as a draughtsman for Carl Hart, and spent the

45

evenings out on the town looking for a break as a performer. Another short-lived day job was as a lifeguard on Long Beach.

At this time, Los Angeles was beginning to define its own rock sound, a marriage of sun-filled 'life-is-easy' optimism and political protest imported from the East Coast, in particular from the Greenwich Village clubs that had given a first platform to the Dylan generation. As the British influence took effect after the commercial explosion of The Beatles, Los Angeles then re-invented an indigenous version of the transatlantic sound, notably through The Byrds. Folk-rock came of age in the city with the Sonny and Cher hits and the extraordinary imagination of Arthur Lee and his band Love. This was the developing musical environment, before it became coloured by San Franciscan psychedelia, that Denver found when he came to the city.

Through meeting local singer Denny Brooks, Denver began to learn about the Los Angeles club scene, which was more extensive than he had suspected, and he also got in touch with an old friend, Ken Ballard, now working with the Cherry Hill Singers at a club in Pasadena called the Ice House. As Denver recalled in *Rolling Stone*, he started singing everywhere he could. 'I went to all the hootenannies and they were going on all over everywhere in LA. The second year I was there I went to Ledbetter's, which was owned by Randy Sparks. I sang and he came back after the show and said he'd really liked my voice and would like to talk to me about working there.'

Denver makes a revealing comment about this apprentice period, showing that at the height of his commercial power in 1975, the time of the interview, his self-mocking humour remained intact. 'Someone somewhere has a tape of the first week I worked there and I think you would be amazed at how – in a sense – how bad it was but, see, I went from being just terrible to being only pretty bad in about five days.'

So it was in Sparks's club in Westwood that Denver first began to make modest waves. Sparks was a major player in the local folk scene. Born in Kansas in 1933, he formed the New Christy Minstrels folk group in New York City in 1961. He took the name from one of the touring minstrel troupes of the mid-nineteenth century, the Christy Minstrels, founded by Edwin Christie [sic]. In 1962 the group edged into the Hot Hundred with a revival of Woody Guthrie's classic, 'This Land is Your Land', and then Sparks and fellow vocalist Barry McGuire wrote the group's major hit 'Green Green', which reached number 14 in June 1963.

McGuire later went solo and resurfaced in 1965 with a chart-topper, the all-purpose protest song written by P.F. Sloan, 'Eve of Destruction'. 'A message record blending folk and R&B. It bites,' was one radio disc jockey's enthusiastic endorsement at the time. It epitomised a new fusion style of pop music led by Bob Dylan, who at this time was preparing to outrage the folk purists with his acidic, electric rock 'n' roll style. *Billboard* ran a front-page lead article in August 1965: 'ROCK + FOLK + PROTEST = AN ERUPTING NEW SOUND'.

The Minstrels had a further brace of sizeable hits, including 'Saturday Night' and 'Today', after which they crept into the Hot Hundred two more times with 'Silly Ol' Summertime' and 'Chim, Chim, Cheree', but by this time they were beginning to lose out to that erupting new sound. A 1963 shot that didn't make the charts, interestingly enough, was called 'Denver' – it was Sparks who was later to prompt the Deutschendorf name change. In January 1965 the group visited Europe, and their bookings included an appearance on the UK's top-rated television variety show, *Sunday Night at the London Palladium*.

Their fame at the time is indicated by the fact that they were represented in Britain by Brian Epstein, at the height of Beatlemania, and when they moved on to Italy they were voted 'top foreign artists' at the prestigious San Remo Festival. Early in the Minstrels' four-year run of success they had relocated to Los

47

Angeles, where they cut their hugely successful album, *Live! at the Troubadour*. This venue was the most celebrated of all the LA clubs and coffee houses, a magnet for aspiring performers, but meantime Sparks was also involved in booking Ledbetter's.

And so it was here that the soon-to-be Denver got his chance, and Sparks was impressed enough to express a willingness to record the débutant. Denver immediately went into Gold Star Studios to cut a demo tape. Sparks's other business interests included a free-and-easy communal house and a second vocal group, the Back Porch Majority, most of whom lived in the house. As a result of his tape Denver found himself offered a room in the house and a gig as the opening act for the Majority.

'That first weekend,' he told *Rolling Stone*, 'I started getting encores and I was extended to 26 weeks there and started getting jobs around the country. I signed a contract, which I couldn't legally do because I was only 20, but I wasn't gonna let not being 21 get in the way so I lied and signed . . .'

Looking back on this valuable apprentice period at Ledbetter's, in a later (1977) interview published in *Family Week*, Denver observed: 'Quite often when people start in music, they are so intent on copying someone successful, or reaching a specific audience, that they lose sight of what they want. I've been blessed because I've never wanted to be like anybody else. At Ledbetter's I was given the great opportunity to find out what I wanted to do, what worked and what didn't on stage, and I found out who I was as a performer.' This is indeed an unusual and, as Denver modestly puts it, a 'blessed' attribute. Almost all the most successful and 'original' of popular music acts started out looking for a voice. The Beatles were Buddy Holly for a time, Bob Dylan was Woody Guthrie singing the blues, The Rolling Stones were swaggering Chicago bluesmen. Denver, though of course looking, listening and learning, was always himself.

It seems an unlikely prospect to contemplate now, but he could have made his mark almost immediately, hitting the high

48

harmonies in The Byrds. It was at this time that another floor-singing hopeful, Jim McGuinn, soon to become better known as Roger, was buzzing with the idea of creating a West Coast version of The Beatles. Indeed, one night at the Troubadour he had abandoned his acoustic folk style and instead offered a set consisting entirely of Beatles cover versions.

McGuinn met up with another folkie who had ambitions to break out of the traditional strait-jacket, Gene Clark (who is referred to in Denver's autobiography, incidentally, as Guy Clark – a confusion with the great Texan singer-songwriter, composer of such dusty-road classics as 'Desperados Waiting for a Train'). McGuinn and Clark heard David Crosby performing his own floor spot at the Troubadour one Monday night, which is when the open-house hootenanny sessions were held, and recognised the third harmony voice that they needed for their embryonic project. They were all ready to move out of the current commercial folk scene – McGuinn had played guitar for the Limeliters and the Chad Mitchell Trio, among others, Crosby had sung with Les Baxter's Balladeers and Clark with the New Christy Minstrels.

Denver tells of McGuinn coming to Ledbetter's one night to hear him. This is likely indeed – their names would have been familiar to one another as fellow hopefuls on the local club scene. Crosby was already on board by this time, with Denver briefly considered as a fourth voice. However, it is clear that the chemistry between Denver and Crosby made this impossible – Denver goes as far as to call his apparent rival, 'the most arrogant, obnoxious person I'd ever met'. And so that, quite clearly, was that, and Denver could not be a Byrd.

Given the way The Byrds developed it is unavoidable to speculate on how Denver might have fared in the group, and on how any subsequent solo career might have been coloured by the experience. Technically, there can be no doubt that the clear-toned new kid on the block could have fitted in – The Byrds, throughout their long and winding career, put the strongest emphasis on their harmony vocals.

As it was, McGuinn, Clark and Crosby performed briefly as the Jet Set and then recruited a rhythm section in bass-player Chris Hillman and drummer Michael Clarke, renaming the band – in clear deference to the British influence – The Beefeaters. They were signed to the major label Columbia, an event that rated two lines in *Billboard*, in a reference to the new 'teen vocal group'. They were taken into the studio by staff producer Terry Melcher, who blended together their distinctive harmonies and a bunch of studio musicians, including Leon Russell, in a glorious version of Bob Dylan's 'Mr Tambourine Man' – famously, the only Byrd to perform on the song as a musician was McGuinn, with his chiming Rickenbacker 12-string guitar. This wonderful record, which reached the top of the *Billboard* charts in June 1965, still rings out as one of the archetypal sounds of the decade. The magazine's review of the single captures the 'trade-speak' of the time: 'The Byrds' sound combines falsetto voicings with blaring guitar chords and a rock bottom drum beat, all applicable for dancing.'

Subsequently, The Byrds gave a rock pulse to folk material, like Pete Seeger's Biblical text, 'Turn, Turn, Turn' and the traditional 'The Bells of Rhymney', and flirted with a spacey, drug-influenced sound – as on 'Eight Miles High' and a later UK hit, the hallucinatory 'Chestnut Mare'. Not all of these were applicable for dancing. In 1968, led along by new member Gram Parsons, the band gave rock credibility to country-and-western with the revolutionary album *Sweetheart of the Rodeo*, which predated Dylan's *Nashville Skyline* and almost single-handedly created the country-rock genre. By this time Clark, whose own writing had given a melancholy, bitter-sweet tinge to the band's repertoire, had moved on to a solo career, and in later years The Byrds lost their identity in a welter of personnel changes. They were always class musicians, though – people of the calibre of

Skip Battin and Clarence White. A 1973 reunion of the original line-up produced a disappointing album, but the band name only really ground to a halt 20 years later with the death of Michael Clarke, who had gained a legal right to use the title and had toured with his own version of The Byrds for the last five years of his life.

Where could Denver have fitted into all this, and would he have had the power to draw the band in yet another direction? Assuming that he and Crosby had got along and that he had become a fully-fledged Byrd, it is hard to see him taking with much enthusiasm to psychedelia or, for that matter, to Gram Parsons's inspired but drug-soaked alchemy performed on hardcore country material. Maybe The Byrds would have had a hit with 'Leaving on a Jet Plane' as soon as it was written, Denver would have left the group even before Clark, sensing a change of direction and hankering after a limelight more under his own control, and the rest of the story would have been much the same. On the other hand could the wild child Parsons and the socially more conservative Denver have produced a glorious compromise, mining a new seam of country music? The purity of one voice, the bruised vulnerability of the other . . .

Country boy John Denver took his stage name from a busy modern city, but in fact it is one that avoids the claustrophobic feel of most conurbations. It is a mile above sea level, for a start, and standing guard on the distant horizon are the exhilarating Rocky Mountains. It retains a frontier feel, a quality that must have appealed to the singer who took its name – the city grew up in the mid-nineteenth century from a sprawl of gold-rush shanty towns.

There was then, and is to an even greater degree now, the further appeal of a lively cultural life in the theatres, museums and one of the finest art galleries in the west, which is particularly strong on Native American artefacts. And in a nation awash with

51

the frozen coloured water that Americans proudly call beer, here is a town dotted with little breweries offering the real thing, and hosting a huge annual beer festival.

However, it seems that the adoption of the name was not the result of an inspirational moment. When Randy Sparks told John that Deutschendorf was not a suitable handle for the LA folk scene's new recruit, various alternatives were discussed and, according to the recipient, 'Denver' was the suggestion 'I disliked the least. I liked the connotation of what goes along with "Denver". The mountains, that kind of country.' A somewhat low-key way to make show-business history, meekly accepting, as he was told, that 'Deutschendorf wouldn't fit on the record label'. Nevertheless, by late 1964 he had taken the first steps on the road to superstardom, with a stage name, a regular gig and a weekly wage.

Until John Denver came along with his Rocky Mountain anthems, the city's most celebrated personality was the 'unsinkable' Molly Brown, who survived the *Titanic* disaster. From here it is some 100 miles south-west to Denver's beloved resort of Aspen, hidden beyond the Rocky ridge, one of many settlements in Colorado catering for well-heeled ski tourists in search of keen air and exercise.

Inevitably, there is a tension, in such an area, between the competing demands of the natural world on the one hand, and tourism and domestic development on the other. Denver must surely have been aware of it from the outset, although in his autobiography he seems to ignore the contradiction involved. He revels in finding an unspoilt tract of land – 'I looked out over the valley and saw that no houses had been built yet' – and decides to build a house on it!

A year after Denver's death this tension came to an ugly head when a group of terrorists calling themselves the Earth Liberation Front carried out an arson attack on the resort of Vail, close to Aspen. As reported in *The Independent* (23 October

1998), in destroying three buildings and causing extensive damage to chair lifts they inflicted damage estimated at $12 million, which they claimed was 'on behalf of the lynx'. Vail was already the biggest ski resort in the country, and owners Vail Resorts Inc. had begun the destruction of an additional 800 acres of forest in order to expand yet further.

The terrorists warned that this would 'ruin the last, best lynx habitat in the state. Putting profits ahead of Colorado's wildlife will not be tolerated . . . We will be back if this greedy corporation continues to trespass into wild and unroaded areas.' Vail symbolises the problem that has developed in all America's winter-sports areas, notably the Rockies and the Appalachians: Denver's generation moved into a discreetly-tamed wilderness, more pilgrims followed, the tourist industry grew and grew, and the corporations involved diversified beyond winter sports into conference hotels and shopping malls. Rents and property prices rocketed, and there was no room in the valleys any longer for those who were not rich. And all this in a nation that has always displayed an urge to destroy nature and replace it with a manageable pastiche – what chance has the lynx got?

One feels that, had he lived, John Denver would have grappled far more sternly with this problem by now. He would have faced up to the contradictions and of course he would have known that the firebomb is no answer. As a rich celebrity with both inevitable self-interest and the interests of the wilderness and its animals at heart, he could have been the one person to thread a path between corporate America and the threatened lynx. One thing's for sure – a bunch of embittered arsonists aren't going to do it.

In December 1964, Denver left Los Angeles for what was originally intended to be a month, firstly for a somewhat fraught family Christmas – clearly his father could not come to terms with the idea of a folk singer for a son. But after that he could celebrate his 21st birthday, which at the time was the age of majority and legal access to alcohol. Then he drove to Houston to play a two-week gig at a club called The Jester. Denver was a success – the fortnight's booking became a month, and through it he got to meet the Kingston Trio, one of the biggest-ever acts working in the folk-pop hybrid that Denver was aiming at.

But there was a price to pay for all this – when he belatedly returned to Los Angeles early in the New Year the musical climate was changing. The Back Porch Majority had splintered into various new permutations, one of which – the Green Grass Group – was headlining at Ledbetter's, while Roger McGuinn had meanwhile got The Byrds under way.

Beat groups were ousting the folkies, and Denver found himself suddenly isolated. It would only have been human of him to feel a little jealous of The Byrds, and angry at David Crosby. As the band rose to international fame with 'Mr Tambourine Man', there must surely have been a sense of 'if only . . .' The old folk scene of Los Angeles, so suddenly usurped by the electric guitars and drum kits of folk-rock and British Beat, had been a supportive, open democracy, with a hint of talent the only calling card required. Now the city was gearing up for the rock revolution, and Denver could find little musical sympathy for the way things were going.

For one thing, British bands were flavour of the year. Of the 25 chart-toppers in 1965, a round dozen were by British acts – precisely 12 more than a decade earlier. Apart from The Byrds there was another ex-folkie who reached the summit that year, a further refugee from the New Christy Minstrels, Barry McGuire. But his throaty rasp and the apocalyptic lyrics of 'Eve of Destruction' were a long way from Denver's gentle acoustic melodies. As for the records that went all the way in the UK charts, only the folksy harmonies of The Seekers, with 'The Carnival Is Over', in any way resembled what Denver was trying to do (although one wonders if he might have fancied a shot at Roger Miller's 'King of the Road'). There must have been

54

moments when he questioned whether the prevailing musical climate could ever accommodate him. In the meantime, he could only stay true to what he was trying to do.

Politically, too, matters were surely getting a little too serious for a happy-go-lucky folk singer – and it is one of the frequent criticisms of Denver that, in spite of the fact that pop music was at last beginning to grapple with real events, he has so often seemed to deliberately stand apart from the tide of current affairs, with the notable exception of his environmental work. The criticism is not fair – he soon made up his mind about the Vietnam War, for example.

In February 1965, Malcolm X, an inspirational leader of the Black Power movement, was assassinated in New York. In April, America invaded the Dominican Republic, and the US troops arrived in South Vietnam, signalling the start of blanket bombing in North Vietnam. Back home that summer, the Watts riots broke out on the red-hot streets of Denver's adopted home, Los Angeles. By and large, Denver's generation of American males were split down the middle – either they were gung ho in support of Uncle Sam's self-appointed mission to wipe out slant-eyed Commies, or they were expressing their revulsion at the war.

In his reminiscences of these days, Denver is candid about his attitude to his call-up – the draft papers had arrived in the summer of 1964. Candid, that is, in his total ambivalence, a confusion that must have affected many of his contemporaries. Although he claims that he 'couldn't conceive of trying to evade the draft in any way', that is exactly what he did, deliberately seeking out an anti-war doctor and demonstrating to him that he was two toes short of a footful, the result of a teenage argument with a lawnmower. Many of us, no doubt, would have been tempted to use a chisel if there was no lawnmower handy, and so certainly cannot criticise Denver's reluctance to spray napalm over peasant children. His denial that he was consciously trying to evade service, however, is curious. He was indeed doing just that, and if everyone could have done the same, one of the darkest stains on America's history might have been avoided.

But there was no doubt on which side of the fence he found himself, and he was later to make positive use of his growing celebrity as a member of the Chad Mitchell Trio in anti-war activism. In this way, out of confusion about the Vietnam War, and out of keen awareness of his father's opinion on such matters, the folk singer found his political voice.

SIX The Chad Mitchell Trio

In the meantime, Denver had to get away from Los Angeles, however temporarily, since what it had once had to offer him no longer seemed to be around. Early in 1965 he drove due east to Phoenix, landing a gig at the Lumber Mill in Scottsdale, just outside the city. At this time he was playing a veritable portable orchestra in the form of an 18-string guitar. It was to prove one of the most important bookings of his career – he was spotted by Mike Kirkland of the Brothers Four.

This folk foursome were a hugely successful West Coast ex-college group, who in 1960 had made the top of the charts, and sold a million, with their début single 'Greenfields'. Though in half a decade of chart success they never quite matched this achievement they figured regularly in the list, and made a dozen or more albums for Columbia. So a word from one of them had considerable weight, and Kirkland chose to pass that word to the top producer of commercial folk acts, Milt Okun, who not only handled the Brothers Four but also Peter, Paul and Mary and the Chad Mitchell Trio among others, and used his artists as roving talent scouts. It so happened that at this very moment Okun was auditioning for a singer to take over from Mitchell in the Trio, since the group leader had landed a part in a Broadway show.

The Chad Mitchell Trio were stars on the campus-and-club circuit, noted for the satirical and political edge to much of their material – Denver would continue this theme at the start of his solo career by cutting 'The Ballad of Spiro Agnew' and 'The Ballad of Richard Nixon' for his début album *Rhymes and Reasons*. The original three, Mitchell himself along with Mike Kobluk and Mike Pugh, came together while students at Gonzaga University in Spokane, Washington. They became professional in 1958, unusually on the advice of a priest, Father Reinard Beaver, who acted as their first manager. The group was completed by accompanist Dennis Collins.

They launched their career by driving the entire width of the country, picking up gigs along the way and heading for New York. Here they played at the Blue Angel club, signed with Kapp Records and began to appear on radio and television shows. The peak of this early stage of their career was a Carnegie Hall concert with headliner Harry Belafonte.

Mike Pugh soon decided to return to his studies at Gonzaga. Among those who auditioned to replace him was Tom Paxton, but the job went to Joe Frazier, whose political awareness strengthened this aspect of the group's work. Then Collins left, and the ex-Limeliters guitarist Jim (Roger) McGuinn was hired in his place. In 1962 the group had two hits on Kapp, the macabre anecdote 'Lizzie Borden' and an anti-racist blues, 'The John Birch Society'. Moving to Mercury in 1963 they scored their third and last hit single, 'The Marvellous Toy'. This rather twee Tom Paxton novelty was revived by Denver on his 1989 set *Christmas Like a Lullaby*, in a version strengthened by a typically fluent James Burton guitar solo. By the time of their final chart appearance the Trio were established nationally as a concert attraction, they were steady album sellers, and were even sponsored by the US State Department to take their music to South America. Then, in 1965, Mitchell decided to move on.

Denver was at the Lumber Mill when he heard of the vacancy, and with hundreds of other hopefuls he sent Okun an audition tape. 'This was far out,' he recalled. 'Here was a chance to audition for somebody I had listened to in college.' He tried not

58

to build too many hopes on it, and indeed was not very happy with the quality of the tape. But a month later, back at the Lumber Mill, he was summoned to New York by Okun to audition properly with the two remaining Trio members.

Alone in New York, a city he'd never visited before, and killing time on a Sunday night before meeting Okun, Denver tells an amusing story about approaching a beautiful woman with the corny chat-up line, 'Are you a model?'

'No,' she replied, 'I'm full-size.' The initial audition went equally badly, with Denver – suffering from a heavy cold – straining too hard to match Mitchell's distinctive high tenor voice, and it was Frazier who persisted, coaching Denver in a couple of songs and encouraging him to relax.

At his second shot Denver performed far better. 'We went back to Milt Okun's office with Joe singing with me and it was a whole different thing.' But Okun had other applicants to assess. As many as 250, in fact. Denver returned to Scottsdale for a tense couple of days – which included being stopped and given the once-over by the police as an armed-robbery suspect – before Okun called to offer him the job. 'His voice was not as good as Chad's, but he lit up the room with his personality,' Okun recalled. Denver returned to Los Angeles to tidy up that stage in his life and then joined his new colleagues in New York for an intensive period of rehearsals – a fortnight's booking at the Cellar Door in Washington DC was only a week away. This momentous occasion in pop music history – given what Denver went on to achieve – rated just one line in *Billboard*'s People and Places news column on 17 July 1965: 'The Mitchell Trio has added John Denver as a replacement for Chad Mitchell, now soloing.'

The group had already been calling themselves the Mitchell Trio for a while. They were billed this way in record-company ads for the early 1965 album with Chad Mitchell still on board, *Typical American Boys*. Now, of course, the new name maintained the link without identifying themselves too closely with their missing high tenor.

At one performance with the Trio, in St Peter, Minnesota during spring 1966, Denver was introduced to a student at Gustavus Adolphus College, where the gig was held – Annie Martell. As he was later to tell *Family Weekly*, he was struck far more by her appearance than he was ever to be by her voice. 'Annie has one of the worst voices, but she sings with enthusiasm. I prefer that to technique in music any time . . . She came in wearing loafers, jeans and an old plaid shirt . . . and I thought she was beautiful.' This was at a student union charity show after the concert, and when 'they asked me to sing . . . I sang every song to her'.

Denver's attraction to Annie remained unspoken – in fact, he hardly said a word to her. But ten months later the Trio were again in the area, in concert at Mankato, 15 miles due south of St Paul. Denver had not forgotten Annie. He managed to find out her telephone number, because by chance he bumped into a group of students from Gustavus Adolphus, and he persuaded her to come to the gig. He drove over to pick her up. 'That was our first date. I courted her nine months and then we got married.'

But matters had begun to move swiftly from the outset, particularly given Denver's peripatetic lifestyle. Annie came to a second Trio gig only a couple of days after the first. By coincidence, her parents had travelled up to Minneapolis for the weekend to watch a couple of football games, and Denver was staying there while working in the area. They drove there together, and Denver met Jim and Norma Martell for the first time.

By Christmas he was sufficiently part of the family to spend some of the holiday period with them, and in the New Year he travelled to Aspen – a fortuitous destination – to meet up with her on a college skiing trip. He was now 23, and ready to get married. At the second proposal, she finally agreed with him.

60

They were married at the Lutheran church in St Peter on 9 June 1967. 'If it wasn't for the big wedding my father gave me,' Annie told *Newsweek* in 1976, 'I would have gotten divorced in a year. John and I really didn't know each other.' Among the guests were Mike Kobluk and Denver's future singing partner David Boise, together with the group's guitarists Paul Prestopino and Bob Hefferan. Denver now had to learn how to balance marriage and a career on the road, a trick he never quite managed. Also talking to *Newsweek*, he recalled the financial insecurity of his early married life. 'We were overdrawn every other week and really scraping. We had one lamp we carried from room to room. It was hand-to-mouth and day-to-day and no fun.'

During the period of courtship, the group had kept on the move. With the undercurrent of anti-war sentiment building all the time – a feeling among college-educated kids that their government had involved America in an immoral conflict in which it should have no part – the satirical side of the Trio was striking a chord among those of liberal leanings. As they toured the country there were, inevitably, occasional brushes with those in the military or with fervent anti-Communist rednecks but, by and large, the group could bask in the knowledge that they were singing to the converted, and that their moral and political conscience was uncompromised.

Back in California, where the Trio were working at one point in 1966, NBC-TV and Svengali producer Don Kirshner were trying to come up with a TV pop formula to rival the success of The Beatles in their surreal comedy films, *A Hard Day's Night* and *Help!* These, ironically, were directed by an American, Dick Lester, who had earned his spurs in off-the-wall British humour by working with the Goons, revolutionary comic radio surrealists of the 1950s. The Kirshner concept was to feature a pop group of loveable madcaps, and the production company were trawling wide for talent. For a while they flirted with the notion of using an established group or individual working musicians, and the

61

Mitchell Trio were tested along with others such as The Lovin' Spoonful and Stephen Stills.

Kirshner soon came to the conclusion that malleable strangers would be less trouble, and formed his Monkees by selecting two former child actors: Mickey 'Circus Boy' Dolenz and Davy Jones, a Mancunian – who therefore forged a British link with The Beatles – and a former apprentice jockey who had acted in the UK's top-rated television programme *Coronation Street*. They were recruited as drummer and lead vocalist/maracas-shaker respectively, and the band was completed by Peter Tork, an enthusiastic mimer of the bass guitar, and guitarist Mike Nesmith, who could actually play his instrument and later achieved cult credibility as a singer-songwriter. With the help of talented writers like Tommy Boyce and Bobby Hart, Neil Diamond and John Stewart, and with the cream of studio session musicians working on the records, this 'instant' group had a string of hits that still sound pretty good today.

Denver, then, was not fated to be a Monkee any more than a Byrd. But, under the influence in particular of Joe Frazier, he was becoming something of a political activist. When the Trio were playing in Madison, Wisconsin, Frazier and Denver joined a student demonstration against one of the major local employers, Dow Chemical, whose products contributed to the Vietnam War. The group also marched in Washington with the black comedian Dick Gregory, who was passionately and articulately opposed to the war – needless to say, blacks were proportionately over-represented hugely in the front-line troops, dying in a country they'd never heard of before the war started, since black youngsters were less likely to have family influences able to pull strings with the local draft board. Singing songs against corporate America, beyond the security of the footlights, was a new experience for Denver. And naturally it was one that exacerbated the rift between him and his patriotic, military-minded father.

Working regularly with the group, Denver gained in confidence week by week. Some of the material he had been performing in Los Angeles and Scottsdale, like his 12-string guitar instrumental version of 'The Bells of Rhymney' and – showing there were no hard feelings – his own interpretation of 'Mr Tambourine Man', worked their way into the act. They were followed by early compositions of his own, including a song about his girlfriend at the time, 'For Baby (For Bobbie)'. A year after Denver's début with the Trio they returned to the Cellar Door in Washington as headliners, and now there were queues round the block. However, the constant travelling and living away from home meant that the money disappeared as soon as it had been earned. At one time, Denver says, he was alone in a Manhattan hotel with tonsillitis and 35 cents, a bleak illustration of the reality of life on the road.

It was shortly after the second engagement at the Cellar Door that Denver wrote the song that was to change his life. Staying with a friend in Virginia, Jim Cunningham, between the Washington stint and a performance at the Philadelphia Folk Festival with the Trio, Denver was alone in the house one evening and found a complete song forming in his mind. At that stage he called it 'Oh, Babe, I Hate to Go', and says that, 'I knew I'd written my best song yet.' Milt Okun agreed, although he insisted on a title change to 'Leaving on a Jet Plane'.

In-between Trio commitments Denver kept his hand in as a solo performer by doing impromptu sets as the occasion arose. In autumn 1966 he booked into Gold Star Studios in Los Angeles, where he had made his first demonstration tape, but this time he was accompanied by the Trio guitarists Paul Prestopino and Bob Hefferan. He cut acoustic versions of 13 of his own songs and pressed up 250 copies, with the idea of using them as demo discs and Christmas gifts. The one he sent to Peter, Paul and Mary, whom Denver had already got to know on the concert circuit as fellow members of the Milt Okun stable, was to serve both purposes.

'I really learned a lot with the Trio,' Denver told *Rolling Stone*. 'They were really professional, but quite often one of the guys would be late and I would go on and do a kind of an opening act by myself. And then when we were in places like the Cellar Door I would do hootenannies. I'd go on and do stuff that the Trio didn't want to do.'

In the musical world into which the Chad Mitchell Trio fitted, a synthesis of traditional folk and folk-blues structures with contemporary material, sometimes with a libertarian political edge, the biggest stars of all were Peter, Paul and Mary. From 1962 and for the rest of the decade (ironically, Denver as a songwriter was to give them their first number one, but it proved to be their last hit!), the Trio repeatedly entered the Hot Hundred, 19 times in all including a remarkable run of five consecutive hits in 1963. In this, their peak year, they just missed out on the top spot firstly with the hippy nursery rhyme 'Puff the Magic Dragon' – unforgettable melody, unbearably fey lyrics (even if they are some elaborate code for the mind-expanding effects of the laughing weed) – and then in total contrast with young Bob Dylan's early calling card, the political diatribe 'Blowin' in the Wind'. The next record, Dylan's beautiful and resigned 'Don't Think Twice, It's All Right' also made the Top Ten. Although Dylan was soon to become the most significant solo artist of the 1960s it was this early patronage by Peter, Paul and Mary that first brought him to wide attention.

The trio were a New York coffee-house act discovered by Albert Grossman – the manager who also spotted Dylan playing in Greenwich Village. While based in Chicago he had set up the first contemporary club specialising in folk music, and he produced the celebrated Newport Folk Festivals of 1959 and 1960, which were crucial in introducing such blues giants as Muddy Waters to a new, white audience. When he relocated to New York he soon became a central figure in the folk boom.

64

Mary Travers had grown up in New York with her journalist parents, meeting such giants as Pete Seeger and Paul Robeson when she was a child. At the age of 14 she was part of a children's chorus backing Seeger in the recording studio, and at 15 she began singing Greenwich Village floor spots. Noel Stookey (who became 'Paul' when the group were casting around for a catchy name) had dabbled in rock 'n' roll bands while he was a student before moving to New York as a manager with a chemical company. He was converted to folk music by hearing the likes of Ramblin' Jack Elliott and Dave Van Ronk in the Village, and gave up his day job in 1960. Peter Yarrow studied psychology at Cornell University but also became involved in a course in folk lore and folk music, which he began first to teach and then to perform publicly. A television appearance in 1960 led to a booking at that year's Newport Festival.

It was Grossman who was the catalyst in bringing the three together. Travers and Stookey already knew one another through performing at a club called the Gaslight, and had informally teamed up to work out some joint material when Grossman suggested to Stookey that he join a vocal group. Stookey refused, but then Travers introduced him to another vocalist friend of hers – Peter Yarrow. It transpired that it had been Yarrow that Grossman had in mind to complete the group anyway. They got on together, settled on the group name and Grossman became their manager.

The trio began work in spring, 1961, and after playing the coffee-house circuit they signed to Warner Brothers, with whom they remained throughout the decade. Their first, eponymous, album produced a début single – and double-sided hit – in 'If I Had a Hammer' and 'Lemon Tree'. The following year they forged the Dylan connection, and the group used their fame to promote civil rights causes and, later, anti-Vietnam War activity. In 1965, *Billboard* noted, with more sense of business than social morality, that 'at the risk of damaging their careers in the south, the trio appeared at both Civil Rights marches on Washington and on Montgomery, Ala.' That year they had won that magazine's award as Top Artist on Campus for the second year running, confirmation that their liberal political leanings were in tune with the mood of youth, even if their sound was beginning to belong in the immediately preceding era.

Finally, in 1969, their career was capped with the help of John Denver and that elusive chart-topping hit, and in 1970 they decided to call it a day. As well as their consistent success in the singles charts they had recorded ten albums, eight of which went gold and five platinum.

Meanwhile the Mitchell Trio were also slowly unravelling. In 1967, the newlyweds took a holiday in Italy before joining up with the Trio in England. But unfortunately, one by one, the bookings fell through, and they found themselves adrift in London without any money. They gave Sweden a try without success, and by this time Annie had given up the struggle and gone home.

In *Take Me Home* Denver is honest about how hurtful he found this, as if not wishing to trail around Europe in search of non-existent gigs was a betrayal. An infidelity, even – and since infidelity was the way in which Denver was to seek solace for his lonely life on the road, the marriage was perhaps never built to last. There was also a danger of it becoming as rootless as Denver's own childhood – they moved to Chicago, but it was too expensive, and to Minneapolis, but it was too suburban. The temporary accommodation in Chicago was an apartment passed on to them by Mike Kobluk, on the 47th floor of the Marina City development. For someone who was soon to find his roots in the natural world this could never have been a long-term home.

Later, in the autumn of 1967, Joe Frazier had had enough, and left the group. He was replaced by David Boise, from Texas, and in 1968 the only remaining original, Mike Kobluk, also left.

Mike Johnson came into a group that now had no 'Mitchell' connection whatsoever, and so they began to trade as Denver, Boise and Johnson. But once 'Leaving on a Jet Plane' began to make commercial waves in 1969, the future became clear for John Denver.

SEVEN

Flying Solo

Meantime, however, there was one further stage in Denver's career before taking the solo gamble. With David Boise in for the departing Joe Frazier the group cut a further album retaining the 'Mitchell' tag, *The Mitchell Trio Alive*, and this contained their version of Denver's new song 'Leaving on a Jet Plane'. During the life of the group there had been a whole succession of management changes. In the time that they were handled by the firm of Chartoff and Winkler, Denver met the company accountant assigned to the group's affairs, Hal Thau. As first accountant, then business manager, then personal manager, Thau was to become a vital part of the Denver story.

When Chartoff and Winkler gave up artist management the trio signed first with Artie Mogull and then with a Duluth agency, Variety Theater. One of the final nudges towards a solo career for Denver was when, because Duluth had been suddenly cut off by a snowstorm, he collected the Trio's fee for a gig at the Air Force Academy in Colorado Springs. The agency representative had been unable to get out on the road due to the weather conditions. At the time the group were being paid $1,250 a night, but the cheque for that evening was for $3,500, making for a somewhat over-generous agency percentage. This sharp practice seemed like a betrayal to the trusting Denver.

He was already aware of Aspen, of course, the resort to which he had trailed Annie on her college skiing trip. And now, indeed,

69

both of them were even beginning to think in terms of living there. He reasoned shrewdly that, with or without any residual celebrity from the Mitchell Trio association, a ski resort would be the ideal place to try and establish a solo career – no pressure, no press scrutiny, no high expectations. He could work things out at his own pace, away from the pressures of the now-famous coffee-house circuit.

He was offered a two-week Christmas stint at the Leather Jug in the tiny settlement of Snowmass, in the shadow of the 14,000-foot mountain some 20 minutes' drive to the west of Aspen, and was successful enough there to be held over for a further month. This led to a return booking, and then to a month's work in San Francisco – one of the other Snowmass club owners had a venue there as well. A friend from that time, Paul Lurch, recalled Denver's confidence in his future. 'None of us believed John Denver was going to be a household word . . . but he did. Even when he was poor he was an incredible optimist.'

It was during this period that Mike Kobluk left the Trio, and since there were now no original members left the group no longer had any legal claim to the 'Mitchell' tag, in accordance with an agreement arrived at when Chad Mitchell left. Indeed, Mitchell went to court to ensure that this was complied with.

The brief career of Denver, Boise and Johnson was always going to be a transitional one, although Denver later insisted that, in vocal terms, it was the pick of the Trio line-ups. But he was already looking beyond it towards the solo career that was beginning to take shape, while at the same time the old 'coffee house' style of folk group was steadily losing ground in a changing music scene. John Stewart of the Kingston Trio was taking similar steps, and the two of them would occasionally try out material together. Stewart was also rehearsing songs with John Phillips of the Mamas and Papas at around this time.

As Stewart recalled, quoted in Kristin Baggelaar and Donald Milton's *The Folk Music Encyclopedia* (Omnibus Press, 1977): 'I had given a year's notice before I left the [Kingston] Trio, and during that interim I was looking around to see what I was going to do. For a while, I was going to sing with John Denver. John and I rehearsed two songs, "Daydream Believer" and "Leaving on a Jet Plane". Everyone sort of yawned and looked pleasant, and later those two songs went on to be number one in the country. John's writing was going one way and mine was going another, so then I decided to put together a group with Henry Dulce, who was with the Modern Folk Quartet, but we needed a girl singer.

'We found Buffy Ford about five miles from where I was living and when Henry's photography business started picking up, he didn't have time to rehearse, so Buffy and I sang as a duo – John Stewart and Buffy Ford. We did an album for Capitol called *Signals through the Glass*, but it sold only three thousand to four thousand copies, and we played the Hungry I and a few college concerts, but mainly we campaigned for Robert Kennedy when he was running for President. After that, the songs started to dictate where I was going all along, and it became more and more personal, and that's when I recorded *California Bloodlines*.'

This, released in 1969, was the first of an impressive series of solo albums by Stewart, who by now had the royalties for 'Daydream Believer' in his back pocket. However, the closest he came to commercial success under his own name at this time was when the topical 1969 single 'Armstrong' reached 74 in the charts, although ten years later a liaison with the Fleetwood Mac duo Lindsey Buckingham (as producer) and Stevie Nicks (as co-vocalist) at long last brought the name of John Stewart to a wider public. 'Gold' reached the Top Ten, while 'Midnight Wind' and 'Lost Her in the Sun' also charted. Until then Stewart had enjoyed one of the most appreciative and dedicated of cult followings, and in the UK a well-produced and long-running fanzine, *Omaha Rainbow*, was dedicated to his music.

On tiring of the Monkees, Mike Nesmith moved into the same field as Stewart, again usually managing to miss out on

71

wide acclaim while making excellent music with his First National Band (and later a version called the Second National Band), bonded to folk and country roots with a rock pulse. Of those working in this area, of course, it was Denver who emerged from the pack in the late '60s as the real commercial force.

By the spring of 1969 the Denver, Boise and Johnson partnership was effectively dissolved. Mike Johnson quit, and Denver honourably took responsibility for the group's accumulated debt, as the senior surviving member. It amounted to $40,000. He formally dissolved the group, took some work from an agency booking college gigs, and as he recalled it his billing as 'writer of "Leaving on a Jet Plane", formerly of the Mitchell Trio,' was now worth a welcome $500 a week. With no band to pay nor partners to share the money with, no road crew – just a guitar and a basic PA system in the back of the car – and no hotel bills when the college had a bed to spare, Denver was making more money than ever before, even if the agency only came up with four week-long bookings. Above all, he said, 'I could see that what I was doing was working.' And so he was ready to make the formal move into a solo career. In 1973, when that career had borne fruit, this previous part of his life was collected on the album *Beginnings: the Chad Mitchell Trio Featuring John Denver.*

72

EIGHT

The Early Albums

Denver's demonstration tape had been doing the rounds of record companies without any success until Milt Okun contacted Harry Jenkins, an A&R man at RCA. In the summer of 1969, Jenkins summoned Denver for an audition and, as a result, he was offered a two-year, two-album contract, attracting a $7,000 advance each time.

This good news coincided with the Woodstock Festival, held over the muddy, chaotic weekend of 15–17 August 1969 on Max Yasgur's farm in upstate New York. Up to half-a-million people converged on the site – the exact number will never be known (but will always remain less than the number who claim to have been there), because a combination of the sheer weight of bodies and a lack of experience and organisation soon allowed the fences to be breached and turned the event into a 'free festival'. Promotor Artie Kornfeld could afford to be fairly philosophical about this financial disaster, however, since he had already covered his costs by selling the film rights to Warner Brothers.

When Mike Wadleigh's gloriously shambling film of the event was released in the following year, the legend of Woodstock was created, and Joni Mitchell's song 'Woodstock' helped to burnish it (though she got stuck in the traffic jam that sealed off the area and never made it to the festival). The event came to epitomise the peace-and-love era, a time of freedom, drugs, music, casual

73

sex and taking your trousers off in public. It was a heady, exciting cocktail. It is, nevertheless, surprising that Denver expressed disappointment at not being invited to take part, even though he was no stranger either to 'getting high' occasionally nor to casual sex. Not only was he just on the threshold of his solo career, hardly a name to pop automatically into a promotor's mind, but also such image as he had was still of the previous era – of Ivy League suits, strummed guitars and worthy songs about coalminers. The denim and saddle soap Denver was still to come.

Even though Joan Baez was nominally one of the stars of the weekend, and in spite of a stoned, rambling contribution from John Sebastian, who was physically similar to Denver, it is hard to see how the latter could have fitted in. Encouraged by a 'to hell with it' attitude once the rain arrived, it became a far grosser, noisier event than the solo folkie could surely have handled. Former sparring partner David Crosby did indeed succeed, however, in his brand new alliance with Stills and Nash, partly by cranking up the volume until it demanded attention. It was this group that scored the first hit with the 'Woodstock' song – Joni Mitchell had to wait a year until her 'Big Yellow Taxi' took her into the charts, by which time 'Woodstock' had also been a success for British country-rock band Matthews' Southern Comfort.

Back on site, The Who caused their usual mayhem, Joe Cocker rasped and waved his arms about, Ten Years After played their blistering, high-octane blues, Janis Joplin screeched and, above all, on the bedraggled Monday, Jimi Hendrix carried out an impossible-to-follow demolition on 'The Star Spangled Banner', a discordant satirical masterpiece illuminated by genius, with the help of lighter fuel to turn his guitar into a pyre. Gentler souls like Baez, Sebastian, Arlo Guthrie, Country Joe and Richie Havens did indeed have their moments, daylight ones by and large, and Denver would probably have had some success in launching his catch-phrase 'far out', but it is still hard to see him being a hit in this stoned, raucous company.

Surely more suited to Denver was the annual Philadelphia Folk Festival, one of the most prestigious events in the folk calendar, staged at the Old Pool Farm in the Philly suburb of Zieglerville a fortnight after Woodstock. After a Friday evening headed by Theodore Bikel, Denver played on Saturday to an audience of 10,000, along with Bonnie Dobson (co-writer of the Tim Rose hit 'Morning Dew'), white blues master Dave Van Ronk – one of Bob Dylan's great influences – British hippies the Incredible String Band and Denver's friend and rival Tom Paxton. On Sunday the weekend was rounded off with a bill including Oscar Brand Jr, Odetta and Tom Rush.

As a songwriter, Denver had made a cautious start on record. Of the 14 tracks on *Rhymes and Reasons*, which arrived in the record-store racks in October, only four were his own – 'Daydream', 'Circus', the title track and, of course, 'Jet Plane'. When he came to give his own rendition of his main claim to fame at this point in his career, he adopted an effectively wistful, resigned tone of delivery, using his supple voice to build smoothly towards the title line. 'Rhymes and Reasons' was also a confident performance, although it conveyed rather fey sentiments about flowers and children.

RCA could have been forgiven if they were a little distracted at the time. Quite apart from wondering how to exploit any financial interest they might have had in the unexpected phenomenon of Woodstock, they had released Elvis Presley's 'Suspicious Minds' in the previous month as the follow-up to the massive 'In the Ghetto', and it confirmed that their biggest-ever artist was enjoying a career revival. It reached the top of the charts in November, to be chased up the list by 'Don't Cry Daddy', 'Kentucky Rain' and 'The Wonder of You'. The King was back, and in the meantime that trade barometer *Billboard* magazine failed entirely to notice Denver's début. The public took slightly greater note, but the album only managed to creep timorously to number 148 in the list, which means little in terms of volume sales to real customers.

In the same week that 'Suspicious Minds' made number one, however, RCA took out a full page advertisement on the premium-rated inside back cover. 'His poetry is music,' the copywriter trilled. 'His music is poetry. RCA welcomes John Denver.'

In announcing Denver's début single 'Daydream', the copy flowed on. 'Poet. Balladeer. Alive and sensitive to human emotions and human foibles. The words he writes (and he writes hits like "Leaving on a Jet Plane") and the way he sings them reflect all the things John Denver is. The kind of a folk singer we're happy to have join us. And you'll be even happier that he did . . .' Pedants will ask for the names of those other hits like 'Jet Plane', at the time his only claim to fame.

Denver must have been elated, though. The Peter, Paul and Mary single reached the top of the charts in October, and shortly afterwards was placed at number one on *Billboard*'s 'Easy Listening' list as well. Their record company, Warner Brothers, decided to take a tongue-in-cheek dig at its author. They posed their paunchy sales manager Dick Sherman, stripped to the waist and sporting a long blonde wig, in a spoof of the controversial cover photograph adorning supergroup Blind Faith's then-current début album – a nude, pre-pubescent girl shyly holding a model plane. 'We understand there are other covers available,' the copyline warned dealers. 'You should not order them.'

Denver was meanwhile building a reputation on the coffee-house circuit, particularly in Washington, where he became a regular at the Cellar Door. At the turn of the decade the third influential figure in his professional life came on the scene. He had a record producer in Milt Okun, a financial adviser in Hal Thau – it was he who had convinced Denver that the only solution to the Trio's problems was to disband – and he now gained a personal manager in Jerry Weintraub.

By this time Denver's second album, *Take Me to Tomorrow*, was ready, and it was released in May 1970. It showed only a slight increase in confidence in his own material, although significantly two of those he did include were 'Follow Me' and 'Aspenglow', both staple offerings in his subsequent career. The former is an irritating piece, seemingly issuing somewhat sexist instructions against a fey, nursery-rhyme melody. 'Aspenglow' is more significant, the first notable example in his catalogue of a song that deals with a particular aspect of the natural world that has struck him. It evokes the warmth within against the winter cold, of peace in a calm environment. The album was respectfully received, but did little commercially – it barely surfaced in the top 200 listing. Interestingly, it included a version of Tom Paxton's anti-war song 'Jimmy Newman', which appeared at the same time on Paxton's own Milt Okun-produced album.

Paxton was a familiar figure on the same circuit as Denver, but he was already a recording-studio veteran – he had his first Elektra album, *Ramblin' Boy*, released in 1965, and the May 1970 release was titled simply *Tom Paxton 6*. And, in contrast to Denver's impecunious experience in London with the Trio, Paxton was also a folk-club star in the UK – that first album had preceded him across the Atlantic. When he first arrived in London in the mid-'60s, expecting nothing very much, he found that 'many of the songs on that LP had been grabbed up by many English folk-song clubs. So, when I got there, I was flooded with invitations to sing . . . This was the start of my English career, which has always run several laps ahead of my American career.'

Those songs included a beautiful love song that became an 'instant standard', 'The Last Thing on My Mind'; a wistful 'rambling' song in the Woody Guthrie tradition, 'I Can't Help But Wonder Where I'm Bound'; and a children's song with a satirical kick 'What Did You Learn in School Today?' This was in the repertoire of another American ex-patriot folk singer enjoying huge success in the UK at the time, Julie Felix. So, too, was a fourth song from this remarkable début, 'Going to the Zoo', a twee singalong that, like the 'School' song, had also been adopted by the founding father of the folk revival Pete Seeger.

Of the two Okun productions, released simultaneously in the spring of 1970, it was the Paxton set that *Billboard* took note of, saying that the singer was now 'ready for pop glory'. But *Take Me to Tomorrow* was another calling card for Denver, who was gaining in confidence all the time on the coffee-house and concert stage. And it was on that circuit that he first came to the notice of Weintraub, at the instigation of Hal Thau.

Jerry Weintraub was a successful music-business operator from New York who immediately impressed Denver with his low-key strategy towards the up-and-coming singer's career, without any insistence on signing a formal contract. Weintraub was 'hot' at the time with another RCA act, a duo from Omaha, Nebraska. Denny Zager and Rick Evans had come up with a transatlantic million-seller in June 1969, a peer into the future called 'In the Year 2525', allegedly written by Evans in half an hour, that dominated the summer radio. However, they would perhaps not have chosen their main claim to fame which was that, in spite of reaching the top of the charts in both the US and the UK, they never-appeared in either list again, not even in the 99th slot. There have been other chart-toppers who never reappeared in either America or the UK, but to become the ultimate one-hit wonders in both territories doubled the dubious honour.

Although Denver was later to think of working with Weintraub as 'selling my soul to the devil', he was very impressed at the time. Weintraub had all the trappings of success, and so it was flattering that he should be interested in the coffee-house singer. At the RCA convention held in Mexico City in 1970, Denver and Annie stayed at Weintraub's beach house in Acapulco, and that autumn had the use of his luxury apartment in New York. While such largesse cemented the bond between the two, the strategy was to encourage the records to build by getting Denver on to television as much as possible.

Adding to the glamour of Denver's association with Weintraub was the fact that his new manager's wife was a singer that Denver – and his family, indeed – had long admired. Jane Morgan was a cabaret performer of considerable range and sophistication – originally from Boston, she had first trained in Florida and then studied as a lyric soprano at the Juillard School of Music in New York. Musical entrepreneur Bernard Hilda heard her singing in a night-club in the early 1950s and took her to Paris, where she became a star. Returning to America she had a minor 1956 hit with 'Two Different Worlds' before selling a million of 'Fascination', which reached number 11 in the charts in August 1957. In the following year her melodramatic ballad 'The Day the Rains Came', written by Gilbert Becaud and Carl Sigman, reached the top of the British charts, and she made further appearances in the list on both sides of the Atlantic until 1960.

By the time that Denver met her, a decade later, she had no need of hits, being long established as a top cabaret attraction. He and Annie were invited to her New York opening at the Plaza Hotel, where she sang 'Leaving on a Jet Plane' and insisted that Denver took a bow.

This was all clearly a heady experience, though later Denver was to refer to the 'moral ambiguities' involved when a shy country boy teams up with a New York hustler. The TV strategy began to pay off when, late in 1970, Denver made a brief guest appearance on the top-rated *Merv Griffin Show*, not as a featured performer but to indulge in a little backchat with the host. Weintraub could see that Denver's unhip appearance, with the owlish spectacles and the squeaky-clean hair, combined with his pleasant, modest personality, was all material to be worked on, a strength rather than a weakness. The rock 'n' roll business was reaching the heights of excess, with Janis Joplin and Jimi Hendrix succumbing to drug overdoses within weeks of each other that autumn. Weintraub – who was later to mastermind the transformation of Elvis Presley into a Las Vegas icon – saw that Denver, even if he did 'pass the pipe around' in song at least, could exploit that section of the market turned off by long-haired junkies.

Meanwhile RCA had picked up their option on Denver, whose third album *Whose Garden Was This?*, released in October 1970, showed signs of treading water. Although the title song was a Tom Paxton composition, not self-written, it is significant in its environmental theme – the darker side to Denver's own gentle celebration of 'Aspenglow'. Denver only included two of his own numbers, 'Sail Away Home' and 'I Wish I Could Have Been There', together with a fragment of 'Sweet Sweet Life' in a medley. He trawled wide for cover material, including The Beatles' 'Eleanor Rigby', The Band's flag-waver 'The Night They Drove Old Dixie Down' and Jerry Jeff Walker's bittersweet tribute to a busker and philosopher, 'Mr Bojangles'. The record-buying public, however, took no notice. Weintraub was playing a longer game, keeping Denver busy on stage and television, waiting for the breakthrough.

When it came, of course, the breakthrough was a huge one – a gold single and a platinum album, between them the basis of Denver's quite phenomenal success in the 1970s. In *Rolling Stone* he recalled the evening that changed his life. 'I was at the Cellar Door with some friends, Bill and Taffy Danoff, who called themselves Fat City. They wrote a song for me called "I Guess He'd Rather Be in Colorado", a beautiful song I wish I'd written. After the opening night at the Cellar Door we were gonna go back to their house and jam and we were in a car accident and my thumb was broken.'

After having the thumb splinted and bandaged at the local hospital Denver finally made it to Bill and Taffy's house. 'In the early hours of the morning they showed me this chorus and part of the verse to a song they were writing called "Country Roads", and I flipped over that song . . . That morning we finished writing that song and I said we've got to record this on the next album . . .'

This incident took place early in 1971, but the album had in fact supposedly been completed the previous autumn, in New York. Over the Christmas period, Denver and Annie made the decisive move to Aspen – as he recalls it in his autobiography he 'figured we could afford our dream house' because of the success of 'Take Me Home, Country Roads', but this didn't begin to happen until the New Year. Either way, his confidence, even if premature, was certainly not misplaced.

Denver cut the song with Fat City, 'and for the first time Jerry [Weintraub] was excited about what we were doing'. Denver even refers jokingly to rumours of sharp practice, a well-known, if expensive, way of hyping a record into the charts – you buy up thousands of copies (although this requires a lot of travelling, since 'regional breakouts' don't figure in the national list) and stockpile them, releasing them back on to the market once the record has charted to recoup some of your costs.

They weren't in so much of a hurry, however, to overlook the fact that the first pressing had an audible distortion on it. Weintraub insisted that it be withdrawn and re-pressed, and it was eventually shipped back to the stores in March 1971. Denver told *Rolling Stone*: 'By the end of March it had gotten up to about 50 in the charts – the first record we ever had on the charts – and RCA wanted to put it back and release something else. Jerry and I both screamed . . . [we] kept at it and it went [on] to be a number-one record.'

But it didn't get that far until the summer, with the help of promotion that included an advertising spread in *Variety*. Denver himself worked on promoting the record at home in Minneapolis, courting the top local disc jockey and, as a result, that is where it first took off. Meanwhile, the album was released in May, carried along by the gathering bandwagon effect of the single, while back in Starwood, Aspen, a family home facing out towards the mountains was beginning to take shape on a virgin site.

The album was Denver's most accomplished and mature so far. One of the homegrown songs had been written a year earlier, 'one dreary day in Minneapolis. I was so down I wanted to write a feeling-blue song. What I wrote was "Sunshine on My Shoulders" – it came out a positive thing.' On the *Portrait* video, Denver referred to his habit of turning around a dark subject to accentuate the positive, and here was an early example.

The lyric, however, is irredeemably banal, though it must be admitted that this is in part offset by a virtuoso vocal performance, confidently rising through a simple but technically demanding melody. The line, 'Sunshine almost always makes me high' reflects the Van Morrison feeling of 'getting stoned on Nature' – the cheapest of hallucinatory drugs – though the sentiment is weakly expressed. 'My Sweet Lady' is also unambitious in scope, though the perfect clarity of Denver's voice cannot be denied.

The album's title song, 'Poems, Prayers and Promises', uses one of his 'core' melodies, a notation he permutated many times. A reflective mood is effectively conveyed, and here he does not rely simply on nature to get high, but supplements its effect with a pipe of waccy baccy. 'I would rather get stoned than drunk, and I've done both,' Denver once stated.

The Danoff song 'Colorado' now becomes a companion piece to the album's masterpiece, the hurriedly added 'Country Roads'. Here the sprightly country picking provides a well-judged adornment to the lyric, and Denver's voice is buried further in the mix than usual, giving a richer texture to the arrangement. This is an anthem with the power to speak to those who will never know West Virginia. Any country lover, forced to be 'long in city pent' as Keats described it, will know the feeling of the heart lifting as one sloughs off the urban streets and heads for the hills.

The album earned platinum status and eventually – two years later – reached the UK Top Twenty as well, as a result of publicity generated in the wake of Olivia Newton-John's hit cover version of 'Country Roads'. Back at home, the original single reached number two in the *Billboard* chart, and one notch better on some lists, and remained in the chart for the best part of six months. A further cover version of a Denver tune was released in summer 1971: Mary Travers, now solo and looking for another 'Jet Plane', recorded 'Follow Me'. 'It's a catchy and bouncy folk-beat number,' said the *New Musical Express*.

In the August of 1971, now settled in Aspen and having made friends locally, Denver had an experience that was to surface two albums later and inspire the song that will always be most associated with him, the autobiographical 'Rocky Mountain High'. By this time work on the next set, *Aerie,* had already been completed – the phenomenal success of *Poems, Prayers and Promises* and 'Country Roads' was already causing something of a backlog.

'That first summer I started to really get into camping again,' he recalled on *Portrait.* '[I] went . . . to a lake across the valley [Lake Williams] . . . when there is what is called the Perseid meteor shower . . . the most fantastic meteor shower of the year. There were balls of fire that would go all the way across the fire smoking . . . I was camping with some friends at this lake [in fact the party included Annie, who seems to have been airbrushed out of the anecdote by the time Denver came to make the video]. Everyone was pretty nonchalant about the evening . . . "I've seen shooting stars, big deal". I was pretty sure everybody'd gone to sleep until one of those came smokin' across the sky and everybody – "Oh, wow, did you see that?" So we were up all night watching the most glorious display I've ever seen in these mountains . . . and at one point . . . I stood in this little grove of

83

pine trees and recognised that it was darker in there than it was outside . . . there was the softest possible, the most subtle shadow, from the starlight. And those two images kinda stayed in my mind . . .'

The Perseids are visible from mid-July for about a month, reaching a peak around 11–12 August, when on a clear night meteors move across the sky on average one every minute. During the month they visit the Earth they move north-eastward night by night, starting in Andromeda, and they've been described for more than 1,000 years. Clearly, in Denver's mind, they came to act as a focus for his growing sense of wonder at the force of nature.

The weight of Denver's success in 1971 meant that *Rolling Stone*, though it usually operated at the raunchier end of the musical spectrum, could no longer ignore him, and in October it ran a piece by Bob Chorush headed, 'WHO'S HOT? JOHN DEUTSCHENDORF'. 'He's not really too hip or anything, and he doesn't look like a rock star,' reported Chorush, 'especially sitting around the pool of a Los Angeles hotel in a Mickey Mouse T-shirt, blue shorts and blond hair that flops over his ears only when the pull of gravity is being particularly assertive.'

Denver is described as 'fixated somewhere in the early sixties . . . pre-Beatle but not yet post-fraternity. Somewhere between stuffing telephone booths and doping, twisting and protesting'. The writer seems to be trying to maintain the hip credentials of the magazine, while at the same time grappling with the fact that Denver is so clearly honest and likeable that cynicism seems out of place.

Denver talks about his rejection of his real name with a tinge of guilt. 'When things started to happen and I was about to get a record contract, they came to me and said, "Listen, kid, Deutschendorf just isn't going to make it." So they started throwing names at me. I was really against it because I know my parents had thought about that and had never really said anything. They didn't want me to change my name and I was pretty happy with it . . . Denver was the name I disliked least . . . Now it feels like I'm John Denver.' That last self-effacing joke seems to confirm that its opposite is also true, and that John Deutschendorf was still able to see John Denver as a commercial device, an actor's role.

Chorush had clearly tackled more devious, more self-important subjects in his journalistic career. 'John Denver doesn't come across as anything he's not. He's straightforward about answering questions and straightforward about being somewhat embarrassed at being asked questions.' Denver describes how radio station disc jockeys, who a year ago would suddenly think of something really important to do when he turned up with a new single or album to promote, were now all of a sudden interested in whatever he had to say. 'Things like that can get to you,' he mused. 'They can go to your head.'

Chorush concludes that, 'If you're good, sometimes you don't have to be hip.'

The next album, *Aerie*, was released in February 1972, and since it only eventually went gold, rather than platinum, Denver self-effacingly admitted that he had 'slid a little'! The set has an appealing country feel, accentuated by some wistful, bluesy harmonica-playing by Toots Thielmans, and of course it includes the masterful 'The Eagle and the Hawk', discussed earlier as the archetypal Denver song.

Two further Denver compositions add to the growing catalogue of songs where you feel that the muse was more effectively in attendance than usual. 'Starwood in Aspen', which Denver identifies as an earthly paradise, is a song of yearning, adorned by beautifully integrated guitars and an intriguing melody, and it is part of his central pantheistic canon. And 'All of My Memories' is a stately, mournful 'on the road' lament that resists the ever-present danger of sentimentality. Perhaps the Fat City chant 'Friends with You' should also be added to the roll of honour. It shows Denver's gift for making his fans feel that they are indeed his friends, a skill surely at the heart of his success, and musically a nagging drum pattern adds a little toughness to the track. When issued as a single in advance of the album, and as the follow-up to 'Country Roads', it reached the Top 50 before peaking.

It is in three cover versions, however, that Denver further demonstrates his growing confidence. Steve Goodman's classic train song 'City of New Orleans' which, in another cover, gave Arlo Guthrie his biggest hit later in the year, is accorded a strong and jaunty reading, while Kris Kristofferson's aching song of isolation and loneliness, 'Casey's Last Ride', is if anything given even greater power in Denver's spare, careful treatment. This is an impressive achievement, since the original is part of Kristofferson's finest album, *Me and Bobbie McGhee*.

The alliance between Kristofferson and Denver is, in fact, a logical one, since there is enough grit in the former's soul to prevent even such a mournful tale from becoming maudlin, something that as a writer Denver could not always resist. As a singer, however, he has the simple strength to reveal the desperation in such a pared-down line as 'Casey, can you only stay awhile?' Intriguingly, Casey quenches his thirst with a 'pint of bitter', a very un-American choice, and surely a legacy of Kristofferson's experience in England as a Rhodes scholar. Denver is also impressive in a slowed-down, teased-out arrangement of Buddy Holly's 'Everyday'. RCA put this out as the second single from the set, and as the one to coincide with the release of *Aerie*. It was predicted as a 'Top 60' hit in *Billboard* – 'The Buddy Holly classic serves as strong material for this top Denver performance' – but could only climb as far as 81.

The reviewer for *Rolling Stone*, Alec Dubro, found few bull's-eyes in the collection, giving credit for those three covers but strangely ignoring, for example, 'The Eagle and the Hawk'. Denver, he says, is 'a troubled, thought-provoking singer who dares to look beneath the surface . . .', but rejects the album because 'only about four songs out of 12 are really worthy of being ensconced in Dynaflex'. The rest, he says, are 'either too wimpy to take or too forgettable to remember'. Even with my wimp-meter on its most sensitive setting I find this a harsh judgement, and would more easily apply it to the mega-selling set that preceded it.

Denver, however, could have been forgiven for regarding *Aerie* as a transitional piece, since by the time it was released he was already into 'Rocky Mountain High' mode. 'If my recording of "Country Roads" made me a star,' he observed, 'the recording of "Rocky Mountain High" gave me superstar status.'

NINE The Platinum Cowboy

Until the Perseid shower experience that gave Denver the inspiration for 'Rocky Mountain High', the album-in-progress of the same name was to be pinned around his intriguing interpretation of The Beatles's 'Mother Nature's Son'. Although the song is credited to Lennon and McCartney, as was their custom throughout the life of The Beatles, John and Paul had long since abandoned writing together by the time this song was composed in 1968. Not only was it written by McCartney alone, but (as with 'Yesterday', which provoked the celebrated and deliberately misleading *Melody Maker* headline 'Paul Goes Solo') he was the only Beatle to work on the song in the studio.

Listening to Denver's version, however, what is immediately striking is that it could have been written with the American in mind – every word of the lyric chimes with his persona. One surprise, then, is that it took Beatles fan Denver this long to get round to recording the song. Another is that, instead of 'sweetening' a song that must have spoken so directly to him, he strengthens his version by singing in a more detached manner than might be expected, standing back from the lyric with an assured technique.

As with *Aerie*, RCA trailed the album with a sample single, but the bittersweet 'Goodbye Again' was another comparative failure, peaking in August 1972 at 88. Denver saw the song as the completion of a trilogy with 'Jet Plane' and 'Follow Me' – they are songs that explore the dilemma that proved to be the central problem of his emotional life, of balancing the inevitable demands upon a famous travelling man with the responsibilities of a husband and father. *Rocky Mountain High* was released in September and the title track came out two months later, when it was clear that 'Goodbye Again' had exhausted its sales potential.

The most directly autobiographical of Denver's songs, describing his belated discovery of 'home', 'Rocky Mountain High' also contains a topical ecological strand. There was a substantial lobby for trying to bring the Winter Olympics to Denver, with the usual financial benefits to local businesses and the assumed prestige accrued from hosting a sporting bonanza televised world-wide. Not surprisingly, John Denver was bitterly and actively opposed to the scheme, which would have involved huge environmental desecration, hacking down real mountains and reconstructing false ones with suitable slopes – 'more people, more scars upon the land', That year, the people of Sapporo in Japan were enjoying this mixed blessing.

For *Rolling Stone*, Bud Scoppa was assigned to review the album, and he started by rehearsing all the prejudices about Denver and his 'inherent blandness', saying that 'he seems sincere enough, but it is hard to sense any character in anything he says or sings'.

Because of this, Scoppa affected to assume that the *Rocky Mountain High* set must be by some other John Denver. 'It's a crisp, muscular album,' said the convert, 'with compelling singing and some of the most powerful acoustic guitar-dominated arrangements I've heard on record.' What Denver had always needed was something to 'dirty up his act', and this had come by way of these arrangements. 'Denver has surrounded himself with toughness in the form of biting instrumental tracks . . . The sound is echoed, treble-boosted in the manner of a Dave Edmunds-type neo-classicist rock 'n' roll mix . . .'

To Scoppa the key song was 'Prisoners', which for him evoked the first Byrds album, though Denver's newest fan could not summon up much enthusiasm for the pretentious 'Season Suite' which, on vinyl, took up all of side two apart from 'Goodbye Again'. 'Even that has enough jangling urgency to keep it mildly interesting,' he admits. Denver also included on the set that early example of his songwriting – which predated his solo career – 'For Baby (For Bobbie)', which had made its previous appearance on the penultimate Trio album, and was about a girl Denver had met while playing at the Lumber Mill in Scottsdale, and subsequently dated for about a year.

In late November, 'Rocky Mountain High' entered the charts and stayed there for five months, reaching ninth position. In the UK, where audiences were just catching up on the back catalogue (both *Poems, Prayers and Promises* and *Rhymes and Reasons* made the album charts in June 1973), the platinum-selling *Rocky Mountain High* was buried. But this was, in effect, a result of Jerry Weintraub's scheme to widen the base of Denver's career into television, beyond his frequent guest slots on the *Merv Griffin Show* and similar outlets – in the UK, those revived sales for existing albums were a direct result of weekly exposure on television as well as the Olivia Newton-John cover of 'Country Roads'.

'I knew immediately,' Weintraub told *Newsweek*, 'that the press would never accept John Denver. There was no glitter, no balloons. It wasn't The Beatles or Elvis. I had a guy singing about mountains, fresh air and his wife. So I said to myself, "Jerry, let's have a ground-swell hero. Let's break him from the heartland and have the people bring him to the press." That was the game plan.'

And part of it, as far as the UK was concerned, was to exploit the BBC's ongoing interest in quality, middle-of-the-road, contemporary American music. It had made stars out of Julie Felix and Diane Solomon, for instance, and annually devoted airtime to the Wembley Country Music Festival. It also featured

91

one-off specials by American artists, and Weintraub secured guest-spot slots for Denver on shows hosted by two friends, Mary Travers and Tom Paxton. Then, in the spring of 1973 (a year later than Denver was to date it in his autobiography), the producer Stanley Dorfman booked Denver for his own Sunday-night series of six headlining programmes, *The John Denver Show*. Broadcast from 29 April to 3 June, and taped close to transmission, they also regularly featured the Danoffs, Bill and Taffy, and the dance troupe from the BBC's main nod to chart music, *Top of the Pops*, called Pan's People. The first show, somewhat bizarrely, also featured the Instructors of the Army School of Physical Training.

A British star guested on each show – David Essex, Hurricane Smith (a middle-aged record producer who, out of the blue, charted with a couple of mellow-voiced ballads in the early '70s, 'Don't Let It Die' and 'Oh Babe, What Would You Say?'), cabaret performer B.J. Arnau, The Who's lead singer Roger Daltrey, Lulu and Donovan. For the first show, programme guide *Radio Times* weighed in with a picture caption – ' "Singing and the guitar were the key to making friendships for me," says John Denver . . .' – and a mini-feature. Denver came over as pleasantly self-effacing, even self-mocking: 'I'm consciously working at not taking myself too seriously . . . I'm not important and I don't want to be. I'm not making a message with my music. I'm simply expressing myself in the avenue that's open to me.'

This subtle way of breaking Denver in the UK worked well, and hence those 'catalogue' albums duly charted. By this time, of course, he was by his own definition a 'superstar' back home, but Weintraub recognised the importance of groundwork internationally.

On the concert stage Denver had by now become the headliner, and at the end of May 1973 he even prompted a brief reunion of Peter, Paul and Mary. In between taping the fifth and sixth BBC shows he commuted to and from New York, as reported in *Sounds* by Linda Solomon. 'John Denver and Bill Withers toplined the second annual "One-to-One" Benefit Concert at Madison Square Gardens in aid of retarded children at the Willowbrook Home . . . [There were] unbilled performances by Kris Kristofferson and Rita Coolidge, Richie Havens, Sly Stone and, as a real corker, a finale featuring the surprise reuniting for the occasion of Peter, Paul and Mary . . . in a heart-rendering [sic] politically-pointed version of Dylan's "Blowin' in the Wind".

'. . . Despite the cruddy Garden sound system . . . John got off on a great set of songs, including his strong anti-war "Pandora's Box" ["The Box", from *Poems, Prayers and Promises*] and Paxton's grimly-realistic "Jimmy Newman". He was beautifully backed by his regular bassist Dick Kniss, Herb Lovelle on drums, Michael Holmes on piano and Paul Prestopino on guitar . . . The wrap-up blaster was the walk-on . . . of Peter, Paul and Mary, whose very physical presence was almost enough to give something of a musically historical feel to the concert . . .'

Once more, the reviewer's choice of songs to highlight from Denver's playlist give the lie to the image of the singer as someone who was always blissfully unconcerned with the realities of the world. The slackness of some of his writing, and his frequent refuge in sentimentality, are only part of the story. His continuing use of political and sociological material is another, honourable part.

John Denver had now entered a quite phenomenal period of popularity, the years that made him the best-selling American artist of the decade. Throughout this time his creativity was undimmed, and so another album was queueing up for release. *Farewell Andromeda* came out in June 1973, and was to earn another gold disc.

The title song, in full 'Farewell Andromeda (Welcome to My Morning)' – at this period Denver seemed incapable of naming a song without bunging in an alternative title in brackets – is a 'la-da-da' piece of trivia, the sort of song that his detractors assume to be typical of his entire output. And, it must be admitted, electing to make it the title tune is hardly designed to counter this prejudice. In fact, the collection has a far tougher backbone, that muscularity first detected by *Rolling Stone* in the previous set.

'Angel from Montgomery', for example, is one of John Prine's great anthems of despair, the story of an old woman trying to construct dignity from an empty life. The John Denver of the mile-wide grin and the cosy TV specials did keep picking these songs, even ones with titles like 'Sweet Misery', another masterly piece of writing, this time by Hoyt Axton. These selections are matched by Bill Danoff's stately 'We Don't Live Here No More', as bleak and wistful as its double-negative title suggests. As for 'Please, Daddy (Don't Get Drunk This Christmas)' – the bracket virus had infected Danoff as well – it is a wonderful addition to the catalogue of country weepies, songs written with tongue in cheek but, of course, performed dead straight. A little touch of yodel, a passage of semi-spoken homily, with steel guitar and mandolin weeping in the background and Daddy slumped insensible beneath the Christmas tree – this is the type of material that the greatest of country singers (himself a legendary drunkard) George Jones excels at. One can only wonder if, beneath the delicious pastiche, Denver heard any warning bells about his own thirst.

There is certainly an element of frank autobiography contained within 'I'd Rather Be a Cowboy', indicated by the compulsory bracketed addition 'Lady's Chains' – however much Denver may sing of love and family life, and croon 'welcome to my morning', there is always the competing tug of the wide open spaces, where men are men and women are complications that simply need not exist. Certainly, as he was to admit, this was one of the attractions of going on the road to him – the road of charter planes and hotel bars in masculine company, the road that killed his marriages. The cowboy song is given an exhilarating production, with drums and chopping, thickly layered acoustic guitars lifting into the chorus, and a resonating echo boosting Denver's vocals.

It wouldn't be a Denver album without a 'big' ecological piece. 'Rocky Mountain Suite (Cold Nights in Canada)' was inspired, like 'The Eagle and the Hawk', by working on a nature documentary with producer Robert Rieger. The subject in this case was an ex-Mountie called Tommy Tompkins, who had spent nine months living in the wild with a pack of wolves. Denver identified the central question as, 'How does one live in nature without upsetting its balance?' Although he can arrive at a defiant conclusion, asserting that 'The Rockies are living/They never will die', he has become keenly aware by now of the constant threat from 'too many people, too many machines'.

Towards the end of the period working on the television project, in late summer 1972, Denver was joined by Annie for what he ruefully recalled with hindsight as being one of the last times they 'came together in harmony'. But at that moment he seemed to be on top of the world.

By now it was apparent that the worldly-wise *Rolling Stone* was converted to the Denver cause, and Janet Maslin gave the album an unqualified welcome. It was his 'best and most balanced album in a long time, and it takes its strength from the expanded emotional stage that he has been side-stepping all this time.' She identifies the Bryan Bowers song 'Berkeley Woman' as another key track to be added to those discussed above, a 'real curiosity'. It describes how a man becomes entranced by the sight of an unknown woman in a rocking chair, strumming a dulcimer, but this infatuation is witnessed by the man's partner, who 'scratched and clawed' him.

Denver could not have been unaware of the message that he conveyed to those closest to him in choosing this song. 'A woman is the sweetest fruit that God ever put on the vine/And I'd no more love just one kinda woman than drink only one kinda wine.' Not quite the theme he was to explore in 'Annie's Song', his attempt at reconciliation.

It might have seemed a little arrogantly early to have put together a 'greatest hits' package in 1973, although as Denver makes clear in his liner note it was RCA's idea. After his smash in 1971 with 'Take Me Home, Country Roads', only 'Rocky Mountain High' had joined it in reaching the Top Ten. And of the three lesser hits that had kept the Denver career on the road in between those two peaks, he decided in any case not to include 'Friends with You' and Buddy Holly's 'Everyday', although 'Goodbye Again' made it on to the running order. Significantly, the two he ignored were not his compositions, and so he was probably advised to overlook them. So what sort of 'greatest hits' were these? Only a handful to his name, and even then he spurns two of them.

As it turned out, the album proved to be one of the longest-running chart successes of all time, selling more than ten million copies. And, of course, it wasn't in any sense a 'greatest hits' collection at all, more a selection of personal favourites from his own material. Denver made a bold decision at the outset – he wanted to re-record the songs. It is a tribute to his persuasiveness and power that he was allowed this indulgence. Re-recordings of past glories are normally reserved for artists in decline, when they have drifted away (dropped, usually) from the label on which they enjoyed their success and so rehash them for a new employer under a new deal, in the hope that the familiar titles on the sleeve will be all that matters. Only very rarely indeed, as when the Everly Brothers signed with Warner Brothers in 1960 and beautifully re-visited their string of 1950s hits on the Cadence label with the help of Nashville's finest session musicians, is such a project both a young man's game and a creative success.

Denver explained his motives: 'I felt that some of these songs had grown a bit, that I [was] singing better than I [had been] four

Liberty State Park,
4 July 1986
(© Donna Pinto)

Golden Nugget Casino, Atlantic City, New Jersey, 1985
(© Donna Pinto)

Fairfax, Virginia, December 1988
(© Carol Blevins)

Windstar Symposium,
Aspen, Colorado,
August 1993
(© Donna Pinto)

Windstar Symposium,
Aspen, Colorado,
August 1993
(© Carol Blevins)

Kelseyville, California, 21 June 1997
(© Carol Blevins)

or five years [before], and that I would like to treat some of the songs a little differently than I had in the original recordings.' And he surely shows a nice sense of deadpan humour when he says that they are the songs most often requested at concerts, except for 'Rhymes and Reasons', 'which no one ever asks for . . .'!

To this, and the inevitable 'Country Roads', 'Jet Plane' and 'Rocky Mountain High', he added his 1965 apprentice work 'For Baby (For Bobbie)' which, as we have noted, did not appear on a solo album until *Rocky Mountain High*, 'Follow Me' from his 1970 second LP *Take Me to Tomorrow*, nothing at all from *Whose Garden Was This?*, 'Poems, Prayers and Promises' and the dreaded 'Sunshine on My Shoulders' from his fourth outing (but not the great 'I Guess He'd Rather Be in Colorado' – another publishing decision?), 'Starwood in Aspen' and 'The Eagle and the Hawk' from *Aerie* and 'Goodbye Again', also from the *Rocky Mountain* set.

It makes for a satisfying whole and, though I cannot imagine 'The Eagle and the Hawk' being improved upon, the experiment is a creative success – and even on that song, the Lee Holdridge arrangement does indeed add an extra element, making it much more than simply a retread of the piece. Denver is now more confident in his material, sure enough of his career and his worth as a performer to relax into the songs. The distancing effect this achieves actually helps to temper Denver's ever-present threat to spoon on the sugar.

As well as being reunited with Bill and Taffy Danoff for their collaborative 'Country Roads' and for the remake of 'For Baby (For Bobbie)', Denver worked with such seasoned session musicians as multi-instrumentalist Eric Weissberg, who played the finger-busting banjo part on 'Duelling Banjos' at around the same time, and drummer Herbie Lovelle. Guitarist Mike Taylor and bass player Dick Kniss came from Denver's regular band, and future member Steve Weisberg also played guitar on a number of the tracks.

Far from being premature, the timing for this project could not have been more right. It clearly found for Denver a vast new audience who had been aware of his songs before, maybe had bought the two big ones as singles, but who hadn't been died-in-the-wool fans. Once the album had coasted into the American charts it remained there for 175 weeks – three-and-a-half years. Even in the UK, where he had yet to score a hit single and where the albums *Poems, Prayers and Promises* and *Rhymes and Reasons* had each belatedly charted for just five weeks, the 'best of' package clung on for 69 weeks. Not quite a *Bridge over Troubled Water*, perhaps, which British fans kept in the list for six years, but still a phenomenal success. Denver had arrived.

One of the senior writers on *Rolling Stone*, Jon Landau – later to become Bruce Springsteen's manager – decided to have a bit of fun in a 'think piece' published in June 1974, goaded by the success of *Greatest Hits*. Picking on the album chart published on the previous 20 April, he developed a thesis that the 'emphasis in the Top 20 is generally on mediums: medium quality, medium styles, the medium in each field'. Mediocrity, to use an alternative term.

Glancing at just the ten top records in the list, one begins to see what he means – though since he was writing some weeks later, maybe he thought of the idea and then rifled back to find a chart to support it. Denver is in pole position, of course, followed by Wings's *Band on the Run, Chicago VII, Love is the Message* by MFSB, Marvin Hamlisch's soundtrack to *The Sting, Tubular Bells*, Joni Mitchell's *Court and Spark, What Once Were Vices Are Now Habits* by the Doobie Brothers, Deep Purple's *Burn* and *Shinin' On* by Grand Funk. No rock 'n' roll, only Paul McCartney's polite attempt at it. The heavy rock is not *too* heavy, the country not *too* redneck, the soul is shallow and smooth, the singer-songwriter is suitably self-obsessed but not *too* depressing, and *Tubular Bells* is the ultimate in elevator music.

As for Denver, Landau decided that the truce between his

magazine and the chart-topper was over. Denver, he said, purveyed 'television music, done least-common-denominator style, for those who like their entertainment free of annoying tensions . . . John Denver has replaced the infinitely more talented Jim Croce as the leading purveyor of light folk-rock-pop . . . John Denver sings flat. He and producer Milt Okun know that and don't much care. Lyrically, his cheery optimism is so one-dimensional, stiff and repetitive that I find it as oppressive as the excessive rantings of any monolithic heavy-metal band.'

Landau saved his last sneer for 'Country Roads': 'He is fortunate that Ray Charles recorded [it]. His version is so good that 20 years from now Denver may yet be remembered – for having co-written the song.' As the royalties rolled in up the valley like snowdrifts, Denver could afford to remain sanguine. Within a year Landau had left journalism to join the Bruce Springsteen entourage – and John Denver was on the cover of *Rolling Stone.*

TEN Annie's Song

In May 1974, while in New York for a four-night sell out of Madison Square Gardens, Denver dreamed in his hotel one night of being 'given' a boy. Eleven days later, he was to discover, Zak was born, and in July he and Annie drove up to the adoption agency in Minnesota to be united with their adopted son, a boy of Cherokee blood. 'I knew he had chosen us,' said Denver of the moment he saw Zak. It was the week that 'Annie's Song' reached the top of the chart, having entered the Top Ten at the beginning of the month. Denver was now a TV star as well, with guest slots on *The Bob Hope Show* leading to his own TV specials, and meanwhile *Greatest Hits* went on and on.

Milt Okun was later to reflect on Denver's mid-1970s success in a 1976 *Newsweek* interview. 'John exploded,' he said, 'as all the crud of Watergate and Nixon was unfolding, when the papers, radio and TV were full of the darkest, unhumanistic things . . . He evokes the American countryside the way Elgar wrote about the plains of England or Mussorgsky put Russian peasant song into opera. I put him up there with Aaron Copland and "Appalachian Spring". To me, it isn't bland. It's great simple art.'

There were signs that, for a while, Denver was occasionally willing to compromise principles to maintain his middle-of-the-road success, or at least to defer to Jerry Weintraub's less principled show-business wisdom. For a guest slot on a Dick Van Dyke show he wanted to read a poem by Chief Dan George,

101

taking a pro-Native American stance, but accepted Weintraub's opinion that 'it broke the continuity'. And as the *New York Times* reviewer of the Madison Square Garden performances commented: 'An ecologist and a strip miner would have been able to leave Mr Denver's concert with equally clear consciences.'

There were also indications that his phenomenal popularity was wearing a bit thin with some people back home in Aspen. A Denver magazine ran a piece headed 'ROCKY MOUNTAIN HYPE', accusing him of encouraging ecologically-damaging tourism and of exploiting the wilderness for his own ends. Car stickers began to appear saying 'John Denver Go Home'. And, good neighbour though he was when it came to helping his local community, not everyone was impressed. A Denver barman commented: 'It's called raping the countryside. Some do it with land, others do it with music.'

Denver was unrepentant. 'It doesn't bother me. My only concern is that nothing I say gets in the way of what my life – I mean music – does for people.' But there were signs that the fame was getting to him. 'I'm being more effective in achieving the revolutionary goal of transforming the collective conscience of the world in what I do than politicians are.' Taken in isolation, that claim seems both pretentious and boastful. Throughout the rest of his life, however, giving the lie to any local resentment, he remained always ready to work for local fundraising efforts.

Following the success with *Greatest Hits* RCA gave 'Sunshine on My Shoulders' another try as a single, in the reworked version, and this time around it was yet another huge seller, going to the top of the charts. But in the UK, John Denver's career only really gained momentum in August, with the extraordinary success of 'Annie's Song'. Indeed, this was a landmark moment in his success worldwide.

The song was written early in 1974 as a reaction to the developing problems in his marriage. Sometimes Denver had to labour over a song – as he was to do a year later with 'Calypso' –

but as he was an intuitive rather than a systematic writer the opposite could also be true. 'Annie's Song', the biggest hit of his career, was written on a ski lift, in the ten minutes it took to reach the summit of the slope. Sincere and heartfelt though the song was, Denver remained constantly aware of the threat his chosen way of life posed to domestic happiness. 'You could admire the design of your hotel suite only up to a point,' he said candidly. 'There were attractive women around . . .'

In the *Melody Maker* of 20 July 1974, singles reviewer Jeff Ward bet that Great Britain would continue to remain indifferent to the Denver charm. 'Usual wallpaper music from one of the most innocuous of artists,' he pronounced. 'Another dab of the cream puff . . . Conservative, fairly harmless, unoriginal balm for the cosy domestic mind.' As was the custom of the singles column, in a nod backwards towards television's *Juke-box Jury*, the reviewer then had to vote on the record's chances. Ward was unequivocal: 'MISS'.

Bathed with hindsight this still seems a surprising judgement, even allowing for the fact that until then Denver had no real commercial track record in the UK, certainly as a singles artist. In September a full-page advertisement for the singer was to remind readers that there were already 'eight other irresistible Denver albums' in the catalogue apart from the current *Back Home Again*, so resistance to the irresistible had been long and stern, apart from the brief success of the two albums the previous summer. But, like it as millions do or loathe it as I do, 'Annie's Song' is surely cunningly commercial, its sentimentality buoyed along on an unforgettable melody that capitalises on Denver's specific vocal strengths – in other words, a HIT.

Sure enough, on 31 August, Denver assaulted the UK Top Thirty for the first time, making the Top Ten in just another week. By 14 September it had climbed to fourth position, while *Back Home Again* entered the album chart at 23. Pen quills were already being sharpened in anger – as *Melody Maker* reader Doug

103

Bowles wrote from Plymouth: 'One of the most alarming aspects about the chart today is the success of John Denver with "Annie's Song". Our defences are down. Watch out for a deluge of limp Denver records taking valuable air-time away from artists who deserve some recognition.'

By the first week of October, Denver had achieved a double first, topping the chart on both sides of the Atlantic, and in America *Back Home Again* had actually rallied, back to second place, having seemed to have already begun its descent. It went on to achieve 'platinum' status. *Melody Maker* had managed to steer clear of editorial copy on Denver until now, when it felt obliged to despatch its man in New York, Chris Charlesworth, to the singer's return to Madison Square Garden – a three-night sell out this time. Charlesworth had to balance his own indifference, dislike even, with respect for Denver's undeniable popularity and ability to 'work' his audience.

'The halo surrounding John Denver shines as brightly as ever. The singer, quite possibly the biggest record-seller in the US today, [delighted] his mainly middle-of-the-road audience with mainly middle-of-the-road songs. It was, I think, the first time I had been to the Garden and not smelled the sweet aroma of marijuana as I took my seat. John Denver fans, it seems, get their high from the Rocky Mountains, just as the singer does . . . Denver . . . opens up his rather uninteresting life for thousands of devoted admirers.' Had Charlesworth known that Denver actually admitted to writing some early songs under the influence of LSD and marijuana, he might have found the singer more interesting.

'These are people,' the reviewer continued, 'who won't go all the way by liking Bob Dylan, and people who want to go a stage further than Andy Williams. John Denver suits them admirably . . . I can't honestly believe that any human being could be so utterly clean and simple, so full of sweetness and light or so devoid of any discernible bad habits . . .

'Every song he sings is preceded by a preamble about when it was written, who or what it concerns and how much he likes it . . . His wife, Annie, comes in for special mention as do his friends and the musicians and businessmen surrounding him. The only discordant note during the whole evening came, in fact, when Denver introduced his manager Jerry Weintraub.

'A man sitting two seats away from me, a sober looking fellow in a dark suit, white shirt and tie, yelled at the top of his voice, "Weintraub's a —sucker." Curious. The same man yelled "far out" and "groovy" on a number of occasions during the concert, assuring everyone around him that he was very hip despite his conservative attire.

'. . . It must be said that the concert was an unqualified success. Everyone who paid their seven and a half dollars . . . got their money's worth and went home happy, forgetting for the moment such unmentionables as the oil shortage, Watergate and New York's appalling crime rate.

'Such things don't exist in the world of John Denver, and his audience are the kind who turn their backs on the realities of life too. Me, I think I'll lay off too much sugar in my morning tea this week. Don't wanna catch diabetes.'

To those allergic to the sentimental streak in Denver's work, *Back Home Again* does indeed seem to be a step backwards after the comparative toughness of *Farewell Andromeda*. But the title track is an honourable exception, the vocal pleasantly relaxed and restrained, the story driven along by a strong country-music pulse. 'Matthew', too, is rewarding, a thinly-veiled slice of boyhood reminiscence. On the *Portrait* video, Denver confirmed that the song was a tribute to his late uncle Dean, who had clearly provided the family friendship that the boy could not find in the comparatively cold relationship with his father.

'My father was raised on a small family farm in Oklahoma, and some of the happiest memories from my childhood were in the time that I spent on that farm. My dad had a very large family

105

. . . nine boys and two girls. He was the second child, the oldest son, and his second youngest brother was my uncle Dean . . . Dean was killed in a car accident when he was 21 years old . . .'

There is a thread of childhood memory running through the entire album, what with 'Grandma's Feather Bed', 'Thank God I'm a Country Boy' and 'This Old Guitar'. Although Denver always resisted musical labels, these slices of country ham do seem, even if unconsciously, aimed at the cornier end of the country-and-western market.

When, in October, *Melody Maker*'s Allan Jones came to review Denver's next UK single release, which was the revived 'Sunshine on My Shoulders', he felt no need to be objective. 'John Denver is one of those totally abysmal American singer-songwriters who seem to have been created with the sole intention of driving me into a psychotic rage,' said Jones in measured tones. 'His wretched, weeping ballads drive me to murder, pillage and rape,' he confessed. After venting his spleen in this fashion the writer concluded with a more telling observation: 'The song is full of relentless, unthinking optimism.'

This reflects Charlesworth's complaint that, in effect, Planet Denver knows nothing of the world's trials and injustices and does not want to know, preferring to operate in a happy-clappy innocence. I would argue that the tonal purity of Denver's singing does in fact mask a darkness in much of his work, particularly the more personal songs written as his private life began to unravel, and that many of the later songs did indeed grapple with the problems he was accused of ignoring.

On the other hand 'Sunshine on My Shoulders', the work under consideration in this vituperative *Melody Maker* review, is surely one of his laziest pieces of writing. 'Sunshine on the water looks so lovely', is not a simple and affecting reflection of beauty – as an example of a song lyric it is as limp as a week-old lettuce. Denver, however, later took some pride in the song, saying that 'on one level, it was about the virtues of love [while on another]

106

more deeply felt level, it reached out for something the whole world could embrace'. Well, if he did sense a deeper purpose as the song developed on that depressing day in Minnesota when he wrote it, the expression seems too simplistic to lead us towards it. All we are left with is the fact that sunshine on the water looks so lovely.

RCA executives would have smiled grimly at the knowledge that they had paid for a half-page advertisement in the issue of *MM* containing Jones's diatribe. But as the sales figures for 'Annie's Song' continued to hit their desks, the grimace would have faded from behind the smile. The reaction of an audience member to the introduction of Jerry Weintraub, noticed by Chris Charlesworth in his review, remains interesting. Someone else, clearly, had already fallen out with Weintraub, just as Denver was eventually to do.

British reaction to 'Annie's Song' and the Denver phenomenon was the familiar story – he had millions of fans, none of whom wrote for the music press. Even the eccentric (and uncommercial) folk artist Roy Harper, a cult performer to whom the cliché 'wayward genius' was sometimes applied, weighed in with a self-serving whinge. 'I think I've done some f—- great work. And I just can't understand why it hasn't received the acceptance it deserves. Until I look at John Denver and that mob. Then I can see why. The mass of the public aren't into being told what's going on. They aren't into thinking for themselves . . .' Readers' reactions to his outburst were magnanimous – let Harper make minority music, and leave Denver for the masses.

At the end of 1974 the *Melody Maker's* analysis of its charts put 'Annie's Song' as the third-biggest single of the year. If you'd like to rack your memory as to what could have pipped it, look away now. Top points were earned by 'When Will I See You Again?' by The Three Degrees, followed by 'I'm Gonna Make You a Star' by Denver's first BBC 'special guest star' David Essex. With a number-one single, 11 weeks in the Top Thirty, and a hit album, Denver had cracked the UK at last. This success was reflected in the album charts for the year. Again awarding points for chart positions, *Melody Maker* put *Back Home Again* at number 21 in the 1974 list. Top, incidentally, came Mike Oldfield's *Tubular Bells*, the musical doodle that launched Richard Branson's business empire.

But the paper itself remained immune to Denver's appeal. Presented with the next single, 'Sweet Surrender', to review in late January, Colin Irwin said: 'Aagh! It's a brave man who plays a single by the man we all love to hate. It's a foolish one who predicts it won't sell enough copies to take it into ye olde hit parade, but I've never denied being stupid and surely even the silent majority will concede this is no good. It's not even corny . . . A wet record that doesn't deserve drying. (Please God) a miss.'

Between then and early March, back home in America, the single moved steadily up to 14th place before becoming stuck. It did indeed fail to break big in the UK, but RCA were undaunted, and booked a full page to launch Denver's next album. '. . . John sings about the things we all understand. And now he's recorded his first-ever live performance album. Two records, five never-before-recorded songs, it's called *An Evening with John Denver.*'

Defiantly demonstrating editorial independence of the advertising department, *Melody Maker* continued its campaign against the singer, in a manner that was fast becoming tedious. In something called a 'Think Piece', Allan Jones called Denver one of the 'drip rock kings', along with bedsitter hero Al Stewart and the unforgivably successful James Taylor. Denver, said Jones, 'seems to have taken over as a mentholated, less obviously trauma-ridden James Taylor . . . full of infantile optimism . . . He's forever saying goodbye to somebody and heading back to Denver . . . There's little in Denver's catalogue of songs that intimates he's in any way sensitive to the complexities of even the most secluded and idyllic reality.'

Although the vitriol was being dripped on to a soft target, Jones had at least articulated a problem that many unprejudiced listeners encountered in listening to Denver – it was not that the singer's world was one without problems, but that he seemed unwilling to articulate and address them. To which his fans would say that they do not turn to music in order to wallow in misery, but to take comfort from positive optimism.

The live album, meanwhile, was selling by the bucketload in America, rising to third position in the chart and being chased by the single 'Thank God I'm a Country Boy'. Clearly this corny cracker-barrel jig, written by Denver's band member John Sommers (mandolin, guitar, banjo and violin) struck a chord in a country still bruised by the revelations of Watergate corruption – it went all the way up the chart by June. *Melody Maker* capitulated to the man's appeal briefly, running a piece from America by Patti Dewing that recognised his quite extraordinary power over his followers.

'Middle America eats up John Denver like a fried chicken dinner topped off with a piece of home-made apple pie. He's . . . selling tickets on a par with Elvis, Dylan and Elton John . . . Denver live is more impressive than one might expect. He has a special knack for changing a vastly impersonal situation into an intimate occasion, as if he may have overcome an original fear of huge audiences by regarding the mass as a single person. He also possesses an astonishingly powerful voice, which soared clear and free despite the fact that this was his 34th concert in 31 days . . . During "The Eagle and the Hawk", the evening's biggest success both musically and graphically, his vocal prowess was positively stunning.'

Here, I feel, the reviewer has pinpointed the two strongest characteristics of Denver's craft, ones that should be apparent even to those who can find little to admire in his cheery songwriting – his quite extraordinary and intuitive ability to turn a stadium into a singalong among friends (and it's interesting that Dewing suggests this may have initially arisen from stage fright) and his vocal power. It may be the comparatively undemanding nature of his songs that attracts his particular audience, but his greatness as an artist lay in his stage technique and his vocal virtuosity. *An Evening with John Denver* was a staging post, a pause taken at the peak of his career, and a confident, relaxed demonstration of his skill as a performer.

This was the peak of Denver's career, 1975, when *Billboard* put him in the number 1 position in four categories – pop, easy listening, pop singles and country albums. During one weekend he sold 400,000 albums. He started his own record label, Windstar. His television special for ABC, also called *An Evening with John Denver*, was awarded an Emmy as Best Musical Variety Special of 1974–75. When he and Frank Sinatra were enterprisingly linked as joint headliners for a seven-night engagement in Nevada, at the 2,000-seater Harrah's in Lake Tahoe, there were 670,000 applications for reservations, which adds up to 656,000 disappointments. The local telephone system collapsed for a while. 'I'm reminded of what happened to me,' said Sinatra of his co-star. 'Once again America has picked out a hero.'

Back home in Aspen, according to *Newsweek*, his secretary Peggy Johnston was spending her evenings forging Denver's signature on photographs for the fans, desperately trying to keep up with demand. The rocky mountain home was gated and barred, with a security guard handing out the photographs to souvenir hunters. On the gate was a notice saying: 'Please don't bother us. You are not welcome here. Thank you!' As he explained somewhat apologetically in another magazine interview, 'Privacy is the hardest thing for me, and I value it most.' He pointed out that too many people did not seem to realise that they were not the only day-trippers who expected to visit him unannounced, and that when 450 cars a day were pulling up at the gate he could not be expected to greet them, however grateful he was for their support.

110

This was the year that Denver was finally embraced by the country-music establishment. While he was on tour in Australia, the Country Music Association named him Country Music Entertainer of 1975, and voted 'Back Home Again' as the year's best country song. Not everyone agreed, however. It fell to Charlie Rich, a hard-drinking veteran of Sun Records in the early 1960s and a star ten years later with such hits as 'The Most Beautiful Girl in the World', to open the crucial envelope. He saw Denver's name and set fire to the piece of paper with his cigarette lighter.

ELEVEN

Heroes and Causes

Captain Jacques Cousteau (1910–1997) did more than any other individual to develop our knowledge of the undersea world, and from the age of 15 his explorations and experiments went hand-in-hand with film-making. Cousteau developed the aqualung, to give divers the freedom to work and explore remote from their mother ship, and devised waterproof cameras and lights. In 1950 he bought the American-built minesweeper *Calypso,* and in the following year, having adapted it for his purposes, he began an ongoing series of nautical explorations and experiments. These included the first underwater archeological dig of any magnitude, and brought back the first film of the deep-sea ocean bed.

Cousteau's book *The Silent World* was a bestseller in 1953, and knowledge of his work spread even further when it was adapted as a cinema feature film in 1956. Among his pioneering achievements – in 1959 he built the first small research submersible and in 1963 he conducted experiments in which men lived on the sea bed for prolonged periods – he founded the Cousteau Society in 1973, devoted to underwater conservation, of which Denver became an enthusiastic supporter.

Although a 1998 television documentary, *Living a Legend,* screened by BBC2 in their *Reputations* series, suggested that Cousteau was an autocratic self-publicist and to some degree a charlatan – faking scenes in his documentary films, for example – it could not in fact destroy his reputation, and if Cousteau is a flawed hero, to many he is a hero nonetheless. After all, even the saintly Sir David Attenborough has admitted that not everything in his world-famous nature documentaries is exactly as it seems.

And those devoted admirers of Cousteau included John Denver, who died before further skeletons – including an allegedly anti-Semitic one – fell out of Cousteau's closet. The key song on the *Windsong* album, released in September 1975, was Denver's tribute to Cousteau and his work, 'Calypso'. 'I met Captain Cousteau and all the members of the *Calypso* down in Belize, in Central America,' he said. As he walked around the deck of the ship, he found that 'the chorus of the song was there in almost the time it takes to say it. During the remaining time I spent aboard the *Calypso* I tried to finish this song . . . and for some reason I was unable to get anywhere close to what I was hoping to say. . .

'And then I was at home in Aspen, getting ready to go on tour . . . Captain Cousteau had said that he would give me access to their entire library to make a film behind this song if I was able to finish it, and I simply couldn't make it work . . . I went skiing across the valley at Snowmass, and all of a sudden there was this incredible tension to get back home and to work on the song . . . It takes you about 20, 25 minutes to drive from Snowmass back to the house and in that time the whole rest of the song was there for me . . . One of the best songs I think I've ever written . . .'

Maybe RCA did not go along with this, since as a single they originally issued the song on the b-side of the less substantial lament 'I'm Sorry'. The record went to the top of the charts anyway, and with many disc jockeys electing to favour 'Calypso' it soon began to feature in the list in its own right, and pushed 'I'm Sorry' – which was also a hit on the country chart – up into the Top Ten. The album was yet another million-seller, of course.

Olivia Newton-John, who had scored so heavily with her revival of 'Take Me Home, Country Roads', contributed back-up vocals to the next choice of single from the album, 'Fly Away'.

Denver commented that the intention of the album was 'to record the songs that the wind makes', an ambition that might be open to misinterpretation and, in spite of this theme, one of the strongest tracks was the out-of-character 'Song of Wyoming', a wistful cowboy song given a spare, echoing production.

This quite remarkable year was capped when RCA rush-released the seasonal collection *Rocky Mountain Christmas*, which included revivals of 'Aspenglow' and 'Please, Daddy (Don't Get Drunk This Christmas)' among traditional offerings, both sacred and secular – another gold album, and the first time that Denver had aimed at the Christmas market.

Not surprisingly Denver was RCA's golden boy at this time and when, in August 1976, his next album, *Spirit*, was launched, the company made it a focal point of their annual sales convention, held in San Francisco, and announced that he was the biggest seller on the label. Even if the only other artist on their roster had been Elvis Presley, this would still have been a quite staggering achievement. As a single the restrained 'Like a Sad Song', an attractive melody but little more, reached the 30s in the charts, and there was a delightful revival of the 1939 standard by Johnny Burke and Jimmy Van Heusen, 'Polka Dots and Moonbeams'. The highlight of the set, however, was 'In a Grand Way', a polite stab at country-soul that tentatively suggested a possible way forward for Denver, towards the Eagles' sound. The album, not surprisingly, went gold.

Newsweek commented: 'Today, John Denver . . . is the most popular pop singer in America. A Denver TV special invariably gets top ratings. His record albums have sold more than 30 million copies. He's been named poet laureate of his adopted state, Colorado . . .' Denver himself had a simple explanation for all of this. 'I'm Walter Mitty,' he said. 'I'm a kind of Everyman. I epitomise America.' That last comment was picked up by *Rolling Stone* for its Loose Talk column, devoted to quotes that maybe do not come out quite right – in isolation, it suggests that John

Deutschendorf was getting a little carried away by the John Denver phenomenon. The magazine also suggested that he dreamed of being President of the United States, eliciting the comment from his father that 'John's decided to go all the way.'

An unemployed grocery-store clerk, 21-year-old Mike Tyner, defined the America that had adopted John Denver. 'He comes from my walk of life – the American Protestant white middle class.' Once he has said it, it is obvious. This is Denver's heartland.

Rock music has developed from roots that have nothing to do with comfortable, confident white, Anglo-Saxon Protestants (WASPs). It came from the plantations and share-cropping farms of the Deep South, where the black singer hollered the blues and hoped to swap the mule and plough for the juke-joint stage and a record contract. It came from that singer's white neighbour, the dirt farmer playing his own brand of hillbilly blues. It came from city clubs on the wrong side of the tracks, where workers from the steel mills and car plants danced and drank to Muddy Waters or Big Joe Turner. It came from Woody Guthrie and Cisco Houston, peddling their dust-bowl stories, and from Bob Dylan's electric translation of their revolutionary passion. It came from B B King and James Brown, black, proud, exuberant, bellowing 'Show time!' And it came from the long-haired hippy rockers, picking up on everything that had gone before.

These roots and routes of rock grew outside the 'straight' world. Either they could have no part in it, due to skin colour, education, resources or a combination of all three, or they knowingly rejected its stifling demands – at least for a while. Who was to speak for the white, educated, conventional but 'concerned' middle class? No marketing strategy could have come up with a better model than John Denver. And he had the innate talent to step into the role.

Although Denver succeeded above all by simply doing what he did best, he was well aware of all those roots that had nurtured

American music, and in the *Rolling Stone* piece he spoke of his ambition to write 'an American symphony' in collaboration with his arranger Lee Holdridge. This would have been a hugely adventurous piece of work combining 'all the elements of music . . . that have come down from our history.' He mentioned folk music and dance, the blues of the plantations and the jazz of New Orleans, the development of both, once they had migrated north to Chicago, cowboy music and country-and-western, rock 'n' roll and the influence of The Beatles.

Had this wish been fulfilled successfully, it might have placed Denver and Holdridge in the line of Charles Ives and Aaron Copland as creators of specifically American symphonic music. Of artists working in the pop field perhaps David Ackles came closest to this concept, particularly with sections of his 1972 album *American Gothic*, which was written, ironically, in Berkshire and recorded in London.

In *Newsweek* Henry John Sr indicated that he now recognised the distance he kept between himself and his two sons when they were young. 'I admit I was kind of rough on the kids,' he said. 'But it was kind of difficult to be commanding 40 or 50 officers every day and then switch that off when I got into the house.'

The magazine described how Denver had subscribed to a long list of modish 'self-improvement' techniques – transcendental meditation, yoga, Rolfing ('the painful massage therapy designed to relieve tension in the body'), aikido (a technique of non-violent response to an aggressor, introduced to him by Aspen friend Tom Crum), his fascination with the Swami Muktananda, the mysterious power of pyramids, and most importantly his espousal of EST, whose guru Werner Erhard was described by Denver as 'a god'.

EST stands for Erhard Seminar Training, and was devised by Erhard (born Jack Rosenberg in 1935) after he had dabbled in many existing spiritual techniques and directions, including the controversial doctrine of Scientology. EST was a synthesis of his own, arrived at in 1971, and as the name suggests was seminar-based. It was originally a highly confrontational process, with the seminar leader insulting and bellowing at the participants, trying to persuade them to 'get it'. And what they had to get was that they held total responsibility for all their experiences, that they created their own world.

This is a concept at the heart of the whole New Age movement, and EST quickly established itself. But it attracted a great deal of criticism, being attacked as yet another dangerous cult involving brainwashing. The response was to lower the intensity of the seminars, and EST was renamed The Forum, in an attempt to disassociate itself with its controversial past.

John Denver, however, was attracted to EST from the start. At the time, 1971, he was still on the first roller-coaster ride of celebrity, and was seeking some sort of framework to make sense of it all. In this, he was similar to Van Morrison, who has always wandered off down spiritual and philosophical byways in an attempt to give meaning to his experiences. Denver became involved in the local EST workshop in Aspen, and then attended its board meetings in San Francisco. He saw it as a technique of learning 'to be open about what you were denying in yourself'.

There were unforeseen repercussions, however. The combination of an off-the-wall philosophy and a famous pop star acted as a magnet for inadequates, some even claiming Denver to be the new saviour. One woman began to send her belongings to him, commencing with her underwear, in preparation for their 'arranged marriage'.

Not only was he already married, but Annie also took up EST, and it seemed to work for a while. It helped her, she said, to overcome feelings of resentment at her husband's success, at the fact that he 'belonged' to so many. So enthusiastic was Denver that he even persuaded his bemused parents to submit to Erhard's techniques. 'I put Werner Erhard right up there with that Korean Reverend – what's his name? – Moon,' commented an unimpressed Deutschendorf Sr. 'At least Jimmy Carter has Jesus.'

And he also had John Denver, rooting for him during his campaign to win the 1976 Presidential election. After the sour corruption of the Nixon era, and the lumpen right-wing Republicanism of Gerald Ford, the Democratic candidate Jimmy Carter not only offered a change of political direction but came over as open-faced, honest, even (if such is possible for a politician) humble. In spite of this, he only beat off Ford's attempt at re-election by the narrowest margin of the century.

Denver's enthusiasm for EST and his espousal of Jimmy Carter came together in the Hunger Project, which – like the EST philosophy that gave rise to it – was to attract its share of criticism in time. Its detractors claimed that the cause may have made its rich, well-fed western supporters feel a smug glow of achievement, but in fact put too little food into the mouths of the starving.

The trigger point for Denver was a documentary film by West Coast director Keith Bloom called *The Hungry Planet*, which he viewed at an EST workshop. He offered to show the film to a senator friend of his, Wendell Anderson, who in fact had been the sponsor for Zak's adoption. Thus the Hunger Project was born, and its anthem was to be the title song on the album Denver was preparing at the time of Carter's election, 'I Want to Live'.

Step by step Denver brought the project through the corridors of Washington until it arrived in Carter's office. As a result he and fellow-singer Harry Chapin were invited to set up the President's Commission on World and Domestic Hunger. But the commission moved slowly, and alas Chapin died in a car crash just before its findings finally appeared in 1981. And the report, when published, did tend to give ammunition to the critics of the project, in that it offered little in the way of solutions to the intractable problem of world hunger.

Chapin deserved a more dynamic memorial. He was a political

singer in the Woody Guthrie tradition, whose 1972 debut album *Heads and Tails* and its single, 'Taxi', had both been hits, to be followed by such songs as 'Cat's in the Cradle' and 'W.O.L.D.' At the time of his death – almost inevitably *en route* to a benefit gig – he was donating half of his concert earnings to the Hunger Project, and his charitable work was posthumously recognised in 1987 with the award of a Congressional medal.

Meanwhile, the move into films by John Denver was perhaps inevitable for such a huge star. The surprise, in fact, is that more regular film work remained a dream for the future – 'Maybe even directing some day!' Denver said with engagingly childlike enthusiasm on the *Portrait* video. And another surprise was the choice of vehicle – a comic satire directed by Mel Brooks's old sparring partner Carl Reiner and starring the veteran comedian George Burns in the title role of *Oh, God!* Studio boss David Geffen cast Denver as a supermarket employee to whom God appears, the latter concerned to assure the world that he's still around and active (although he gives the appearance of having retired to the golf course). To an extent the movie is an elaborate stand-up routine for the peerless Burns, making barbed observations about modern life. Given the track record of cinematic pop-star vehicles, most notably Elvis Presley's 'lost decade', Denver's screen debut was an impressive one, and it was comfortably successful at the box office.

This was clearly a direction towards which Jerry Weintraub had set his sights, with or without Denver. After their partnership had dissolved in recriminations in 1984, Denver was less than complimentary about Weintraub's involvement, rueing the fact that he had been talked into a percentage deal split 50/50 between them on the film, and wondering what Weintraub had done to deserve a 'producer' credit. Their relationship was to falter when Weintraub seemed to be too busy setting up Holly-wood deals to look after his major star.

Denver came to resent the fact that Weintraub had founded

his own success on that of his star signing, but was now using Denver's name more to further his own career in other directions. He used his power as concert promoter for the country's biggest solo attraction to sign exclusive concert deals with other huge clients, notably Elvis Presley and Frank Sinatra, through his organisation Concerts West.

Late in 1976, Denver toured Japan, his first visit since what he described as 'a forgotten part of my childhood', and was working on *Oh, God!* when he and Annie heard from the adoption agency about their second child, a Japanese–American baby who was to be called Anna Kate. They had to survive stern questioning about the state of their marriage before the procedure was allowed to go ahead.

Early in 1977, RCA deemed the time to be right for a second volume of the *Greatest Hits*, drawn from the 'regular' albums from *Farewell Andromeda* onwards. Of course it sold, but whereas the first hits collection, at least in hindsight, proved to be a significant stepping-stone in establishing Denver as one of the biggest artists of all time, he had surely now reached the point where the whole world, or at least that part of the world likely to be interested, had the original albums anyway.

However, Denver had also arrived at a stage of some confusion in his career, partly and ironically as a direct result of his remarkable success, and so RCA's motive was simply to get 'product' into the racks – they weren't able to release another new set of songs until November. Denver referred to this confusion as a 'veering' in all his relationships – with his music, the band, his manager, his wife, 'even the sense I had of myself as a human being. The changes began then and continued with increasing complication, through the next four or five years.' He chose a striking image, a metaphor drawn from his own experience, to describe the feeling that at one moment everything seemed to be going just right, and then suddenly it wasn't any more. 'It was as if I was flying along and then the plane flipped.'

Denver could feel his music changing, growing away from its former self, and this affected his attitude to the band, who are after all the closest a musician on the road has to a family. Guitarist Mike Taylor and bass-player Dick Kniss had joined him in the Cellar Door days with Bill and Taffy Danoff, up to and beyond the time that 'Country Roads' took off. In the mid-'70s Taylor left and a couple of 'Aspenites' came into the group, Steve Weisberg as a direct replacement for Taylor and multi-instrumentalist John Sommers to augment the sound.

Now, in 1977, Denver decided that he had to part with Weisberg, who he claimed was in the habit of turning up late to recording sessions, and then invariably wanting to try another take after everyone else was satisfied and exhausted. And as he worked on the next 'proper' album, to be called *I Want to Live,* Denver further came to the conclusion that Kniss wasn't right for the sounds that he could hear in his head. When such peerless session players as James Burton, the greatest of all country-rock guitarists, and his long-time partner and piano player Glen D. Hardin, were brought in to the picture, the only remaining member of the earlier band, Sommers, felt intimidated by their prowess. And so he too called it a day.

Denver's response was to increase the size of the band to seven musicians, as well as augmenting the back-up singers. Alas, a year later Sommer joined the list of lost friends – he was invited back to sit in for a couple of gigs for old time's sake and, according to Denver, enjoyed it so much that he entertained ideas of not only returning, but of becoming the band leader. This did not fit in with Denver's plans.

He saw the late 1970s as a constant tour, city to city, country to country, a situation that can only threaten home life and a settled marriage. He was willing to admit that this choice of lifestyle was a form of 'running away' – an escape from the hard work needed to make an intimate relationship work, from the day-to-day hassles of running a home, in favour of the camaraderie of the road, with its glitz, shared humour and flattery, its booze and drugs with no domestic disapproval nor late arrivals for family dinner, and with its succession of admiring and available women.

He also carelessly gathered the wrong kind of publicity on one occasion, at a press conference in Sydney, though it could perhaps have increased his standing among those too hip to consider buying a Denver record up until that point. When asked, 'Do you smoke hash?' he replied flippantly: 'Every chance I get.' His 'drug confession' made tabloid headlines around the world. The paranoid Denver flushed the band's entire stash down the lavatory, not a popular move. On the following day he was given a ticket by a traffic cop for riding a motorcycle without a helmet, and on the day after that he rode the wrong way down a one-way street. The omens were getting to him.

One possible salvation for Denver, psychologically at least, was the growing concept of the Windstar Foundation. This was the dream scheme of Denver and his friend Tom Crum. Road manager Kris O'Connor had introduced them when Crum was running a martial arts school in Aspen. Denver soon hired Crum as his personal trainer, and the latter soon joined the entourage on the road.

Windstar was conceived as a gathering-together of knowledge directed at living in harmony with nature, and intended to focus its efforts on studies into energy channelled from the wind and the sun. Its aims were solemnly stated as being to provide 'on-site educational programs in renewable energy and food production techniques, land stewardship and global resource management, conflict resolution, international citizen exchange, and personal and community growth.'

In 1976 Denver bought 1,000 acres near Snowmass as Windstar's base, and Crum became its day-to-day director. They were joined on its board by Hal Thau, to keep an educated eye on the accounts. Inevitably, however, this was a set-up that spent money without earning any, certainly in its formative period. Denver came to think of it as a treadmill needing more than $2 million of his money every year to keep it turning. But, he reasoned, he had six albums in the charts so what the hell.

And with Denver to bankroll it, Windstar prospered. In the late '80s it launched the Windstar Connection Program, designed to spread its work throughout the country. Said its then development director Tyler Norris: 'The purpose is for Windstar members to meet, network and produce events, forums and workshops which educate and inspire people to take responsible action.' Denver's particular interest, exemplified in a seminar he hosted called 'Higher Ground', was to spread information as the basis of effective action, to make sure people were aware of current environmental concerns, to elicit commitment to improvement.

He clearly had support at the highest level – on 18 April 1977, President Carter addressed the nation on television specifically about what he perceived as an energy crisis, one that could develop into a 'national catastrophe', to address which he set goals for reduction in energy consumption. Later Denver was to make his first trip to Africa, at Carter's bidding, as part of a delegation from the Hunger Project – an experience that was to inspire the song 'African Sunrise' on his 1985 album *Dreamland Express*.

In 1977 Denver met Buckminster Fuller for the first time, a hero like Cousteau. A year later they met up again in Denver, where Fuller was promoting his latest book *Critical Path*. Denver found himself on stage interviewing Fuller at a promotional event, and in the evening he and Crum told the guru about their hopes for Windstar.

Fuller, born in Massachusetts in 1895, was a unique figure in American culture, a revolutionary architect with no formal training, an inventor and philosopher. In his work he strove to form an alliance between technology and nature, and in 1947 this led him to perfect his most celebrated innovation, the geodesic dome. This was the culmination of a concept that had seen its earliest hints, perhaps, in Sir Joseph Paxton's glass structure the Crystal Palace, built in London for the Great Exhibition of 1851.

The geodesic dome is a sphere, or more practically a hemisphere, built up of tetrahedrons – three-dimensional shapes with four triangular sides. This shape is found in nature; in crystals, for instance, within the eye's cornea, even in certain viruses. As a building technique the dome demonstrates the maxim 'more with less', and is the perfect realisation of Fuller's philosophy that he called dymaxion, the maximum advantage gained from the minimum input of energy.

A sphere encloses the biggest possible space with the smallest surface area, and is the strongest shape in resisting pressures from inside or out. In addition, a structure of interlocking tetrahedrons has a stability far in excess of that suggested by the actual bulk of the 'bricks' involved. Thus the geodesic dome, once described as 'the most significant structural innovation of the twentieth century', is the most versatile and economical of building forms, and is the neatest demonstration of Fuller's aim to make technology and nature run in harmony.

His most prestigious commission was to design the US Pavilion at the 1967 World's Fair in Montreal, Expo '67, though at the time the largest such dome in the world had a more pragmatic purpose, to enclose the repair shop of the Union Tank Car Company in Baton Rouge, Louisiana. Ultimately, Fuller's vision went beyond industrial plants and sports stadiums to enclose complete cities, the smiling inhabitants living beneath a benign, controlled climate.

Fuller's inventions and philosophies, of which the dome was simply the most celebrated, earned him guru status by the 1960s, and Denver would have seen a link between the avuncular genius and his own hopes for Windstar. On impulse, he and Crum persuaded Fuller to visit the Snowmass site. The latter treated the Windstar staff to an impromptu seminar on his philosophy, and agreed to join the Windstar board. Since such invitations were showered upon Fuller, Denver was sensible of the honour bestowed upon the Windstar ideal. Its first prospectus stated that the 'planet Earth is a living, breathing organism whose vitality, beauty and growth depend on its ability to exist as a unified and harmonious whole'.

Denver himself found a felicitous phrase to describe Windstar's aims – they should be directed at learning 'to live lightly on the planet'. He was perhaps the only owner of a Lear jet, let alone one with turquoise and orange trim, ever to express this sentiment.

Fuller helped to refocus Windstar as a collection of 'information gatherers, pragmatists pulling together what's available to create whatever Spaceship Earth needs to move where the universe is moving'. This chimed with the inspirational title of his 1969 book, *Operating Manual for Spaceship Earth*. After a benign and hugely influential life, Buckminster Fuller left the spaceship in 1983.

With the world's biggest pop star throwing whatever energy he had left after touring the globe into such projects as Windstar and political lobbying, there was now even less room for his marriage. Annie began more and more to build her own social life in Aspen without Denver, who came to feel that he was returning to his own home as an intruder. It could perhaps be said that of the world's major pop musicians only Paul McCartney solved this dilemma, by rigorously placing family ahead of work in his list of priorities. Even then, since one way was to appoint Linda to his band, fans were divided on the results.

TWELVE

The Late 1970s

What was it that John Denver's audience had been buying into during these years of phenomenal success? The Denver image at this time was so wholesome that in 1977 even the middle-America journal *Family Weekly* could happily refer to criticisms of his music as being 'insipid as a vanilla milkshake'. But there was clearly quite a taste for milkshake, given Denver's phenomenal record sales. And since the public in their millions supported this image, he was shrewd enough not to disturb it with too many outrageous quotes. When he made that flippant and instantly notorious remark about smoking grass 'every chance I get' his real self showed through for a moment, and caused a sensation, but by and large he always remained aware of the differences between himself and 'John Denver'. The real self drank, towards the end of his life sometimes to excess, and took recreational drugs, as did almost every musician out there in the no-man's-land of the road. 'John Denver', on the other hand, got high looking at the sunset.

As if he had learned his lesson from that Australian press conference, he was now careful to blur the distinction between self and image. 'I feel there is truth in my music,' he said to *Family Weekly*. 'Truth presented in a way that has no restrictions on it. I would like to be a catalyst. I would like my life to be so true and so honest a reflection of me that people see themselves.' Examined even casually, this seems to be a fine and respectable way of saying absolutely nothing, of frightening no horses, of hitting the 'truth' and 'honesty' triggers without accepting too much responsibility – after all, this is what he says he *feels*, what he would *like* to be true, not what he boasts to have achieved. It was in this interview that he made the comment, noted earlier, that during his younger days he was lucky in not wanting to sound like someone else. He absorbed influence, but did not reproduce it.

Some of the most successful singers of recent decades have motored discreetly along in the middle of the road, and can arrive at vast popularity after a somewhat grittier youth. Neil Diamond, who began as a Brill Building writer peddling his songs to such groups as Jay and the Americans and The Monkees, turned to more ingenious craftsmanship with statements like 'I Am . . . I Said', and rubbed shoulders with The Band and Martin Scorsese, before settling for stardom as a medallion-chested Las Vegas balladeer. Denver was a 'protest' singer in his folk-club days, and the ultimate mums' favourite, Barry Manilow, began as a pianist in a gay bath-house.

These three giants appeal, above all, to a female audience, and offer them – what? Sex appeal without danger? Or with just a hint of danger? Solid musical values in a world of punks and posers? Certainly a sense of predictability, of security, must come into the equation. Whereas a rock artist like David Bowie can tease his audience through a series of adopted personae, the attraction of John Denver must surely be, at least in part, that one can feel certain he is not suddenly going to start cross-dressing, or accept a role in *The Rocky Horror Show*.

Bob Dylan's audience during his greatest years always wanted to be challenged – by the electric folkie, the stream-of-consciousness poet, the country crooner, the stadium rocker – but Denver's did not. Although he lived long enough to go beyond the cutesy hairstyle, and gained a little ruggedness in middle age, not too much else changed. He developed little as an artist, although certainly he became more and more focused

128

on his particular environmental concerns, and he was never going to become a rocker or a renegade. As writer Lou Carlozo observed in *Chicago Tribune*, 'even Donny Osmond is a little bit rock 'n' roll by comparison'. Denver, of course, had no reason at all to be disturbed by such comments, and put it down to city prejudice. He knew what he did well, and fortunately it was exactly what he wanted to do, and exactly what his vast audience also wanted him to do.

In the meantime, Denver's relationship with his father was showing some improvement towards the end of the older man's life. This was partly a natural result of the singer's extraordinary success in his chosen career, and he bolstered this by bringing his parents to concerts and television shows whenever possible, so that they could see, even bask in, his popularity for themselves. This in itself, though, did not necessarily bring father and son any closer together emotionally.

Aircraft, however, offered the chance of forging a closer bond. Denver had first sensed the fascination of flying when he was invited into the cockpit of a chartered plane flying home to Minneapolis from Ohio, and he realised that, after all, it was in his blood. He signed up for lessons after the move to Aspen with Annie and he progressed swiftly, first flying solo after just a few hours of tuition.

When Denver bought the first plane of his own, a Cessna, the insurance policy decreed that he should fly for 50 hours in dual control with another qualified pilot before being allowed to take sole charge. The obvious co-pilot was in the family, and his father took to the role with enthusiasm. He taught his son that the key to flying a small plane is to make it do what you want it to do, to be truly in command of the machinery. With the older man as tutor, the natural pecking order between father and son was restored, an order that – in spite of Henry John Sr's huge standing within his profession – is hard to maintain when your son is the world's biggest pop star.

Once Denver was bitten by the flying bug, however, it was yet another reason to be away from home. It was not that he was unaware of the problem, more that it was a problem that snowballed until it seemed to loom too large to eradicate. In 1975 he had told *Rolling Stone*: 'I need to have some time at home . . . I need it for me in regard to me and Annie . . . in regard to me and my little boy . . . in regard to me and the universe.'

And yet having acknowledged this need with such pretentious hyperbole he was immediately off on another tack. 'I'm involved with the Bicentennial Commission in Colorado and I want to get involved with [it] on a national level. What I would like to do . . . is to get through to young people . . . and to open up the space for them to take a look at who we are . . . The thing about it is it's not going to cost any money, and we're spending millions and millions of dollars on stuff for this bicentennial, some of which I think is a total waste.' His laudable ambitions were not helped by the choice of quoted examples – to get the kids planting flowers and keeping the streets clean.

With the second volume of 'hits' keeping Denver in the record racks throughout 1977, and *Oh, God!* doing very healthy business, the next studio album did not appear until November, 15 months after *Spirit*. Called *I Want to Live*, which was formerly the title of a 1958 anti-capital punishment movie starring Susan Hayward, it took its name from the collection's most significant song, the one Denver had written for the Hunger Project. This telling piece of agitprop gave some substance to an otherwise disappointing set. Denver's skill in casting fresh light on the songs of others did not extend to his version of Eric Andersen's 'Thirsty Boots', for example. Andersen, a leading light of the Greenwich Village club scene since his arrival there in 1964, is best remembered for this charming song, a hit for Judy Collins, and for the much-covered 'Violets of Dawn', which had given its name to a Mitchell Trio album. But Denver gives 'Thirsty Boots' a somewhat listless interpretation.

The album's other main point of interest is in a pair of songs that reflect the warring sides of Denver's nature at the time. 'How Can I Leave You Again?', with its rueful follow-up line 'I must be out of my mind', is another number that attempts to address the problem of maintaining a personal relationship when the singer is always leaving to go back on the road. Like Denver the husband, Denver the songwriter can come to no satisfactory resolution.

The companion piece was written not by Denver but by Jimmy Ibbotson of the Nitty Gritty Dirt Band, with whom Denver later worked when they cut the follow-up to their majestic anthology of country-music styles, *Will the Circle Be Unbroken?* Called 'Ripplin' Waters', the song is a celebration of domestic harmony amid the beauties of nature, a goal that Denver had within his grasp but always seemed fated to let slip. As the track approaches its fade-out, the bass line briefly echoes the melody of 'How Can I Leave You Again?', as if to stress the ironic link between the two songs.

After 14 original albums Denver finally got round to calling one *John Denver*, strangely hurried out by RCA in January 1978. It has a transitional feel to it, as well as an uncertainty of direction – from a stab at 'Johnny B. Goode' to the nursery-rhyme feyness of 'Garden Song'. Denver seems more at home with a straightforward love song like 'You're So Beautiful', which builds up a fair head of steam, and his reflective interpretation of the melodic Herb Pedersen song 'Southwind' is impressive.

With his environmental concerns and concert tours taking precedence, Denver did not record again until 1979, when he flew to London to forge an alliance that did nothing for his credibility rating among the unconverted. *A Christmas Together,* released in October, teamed him with Jim Henson's repertory company of anarchic dolls, The Muppets, then at the height of their television fame.

The separation from Annie that this project necessitated reduced Denver to a low ebb of depression at total odds with the light-hearted and gimmicky nature of the album he was working on, and he even toyed with the idea of suicide. This brought him to the realisation that his marriage was worth saving, and in between stilted, cold telephone calls back home to Aspen he wrote one of his most directly personal songs ever. 'In My Heart', which was to adorn his next album in due course, is an attempt in part to make sense of a marriage often conducted on two separate continents. Its heartfelt nature, its birth in desperation, makes it a far deeper piece of work than Denver normally attempted. 'It was meant as a gift,' he said forlornly, 'but I don't think Annie ever unpacked it.'

The album, its personal nature stressed by the chosen title *Autograph*, carried Denver impressively into the 1980s after a period of treading water and messing around with puppets. His voice had shaken off its recent tendency towards listlessness, and he attacked the set with a new-found conviction. As a reflection of his life at the time, the album mixed personal and environmental concerns. If he still wished to resist being tagged as a country singer, however, then Rodney Crowell's majestic anthem 'Song for the Life' was a strange choice of material. Crowell was one of the new breed of writers who at the time were kicking a little much-needed rock 'n' roll spirit into Nashville, and Denver gives the song a rousing treatment.

By now Denver was clear that he wanted his marriage to work, and the title song of the album could hardly be a more direct affirmation of this, another heartfelt attempt at reconciliation. He tried to improve matters by appointing Annie to the board of the Windstar Foundation, to involve her in one of his obsessions. But when people begin to grow apart the most apparently trivial causes of tension can also be the most fundamental. Denver, having spent so many years rummaging through the grab-bag of New Age theories, had come to believe that by sticking to a macrobiotic diet when out on the road he felt much more energised, a much fitter person. Macrobiotics, founded in Zen Buddhism, is based on the purity of naturally-grown vegetables. When he came home to Aspen he decided that his wife's more imaginative cooking, with its rich sauces, made him feel sluggish. The table, the breaking of bread, is surely at the very centre of home life, and so to fall out over food strikes dangerously at the heart of domesticity.

THIRTEEN

John Denver Versus RCA

Out in Los Angeles in the summer of 1980, and in some confusion, Denver was attempting to work with Milt Okun on the next album. At one stage he sought help and advice from the guru Swami Muktananda, who had an ashram up in Oakland, just across the bay from San Francisco proper. Denver's state of mind at the time was not just caused by the growing estrangement from Annie, but also by the band – not for reasons of personality conflict but because, like John Sommers before him, he was beginning to feel somewhat intimidated by the casual professionalism of such consummate musicians.

One day, instead of reporting to the studio in Los Angeles, he played truant and drove north towards the coastal town of Big Sur, down the coast from Monterey. Okun had been asking him for another love song to balance the album they had been working on, and it suddenly came, almost unforced – 'Perhaps Love'.

But instead of solving the problem of completing the next set of songs, 'Perhaps Love' became part of the problem. There had been management changes at RCA, with younger, more country-oriented people coming in and replacing those who had formed a personal line of contact with Denver. The new regime looked at the books and saw that they were still committed to paying Denver $1 million advance for each album, even though his sales were in decline – perhaps inevitably, since his reign as the company's all-time biggest seller could hardly have continued indefinitely. The company men listened to what Denver and Okun had produced in Los Angeles, and rejected it. Not up to standard, they said, which of course begs the question as to whether they would ever be minded to be sympathetic to his music again, whatever the standard.

Jerry Weintraub attempted to go along with the new thinking at RCA. He dispensed with the services of Okun, the man who had 'created' the Denver sound, and despatched the singer to Nashville in the hope of turning him into the kind of country singer that the record company wanted. Songs like 'Perhaps Love' did not fit into the scheme. Meanwhile, Okun's reputation as a producer ensured that the telephone soon rang, and Columbia Records hired him to turn Placido Domingo into a pop singer.

He offered 'Annie's Song' to the opera star, and 'Perhaps Love' as well. His first idea was to bring together Domingo and the Irish fluter James Galway, who had reached the UK Top Ten with his version of 'Annie's Song', with Denver pitching in on guitar. When this scheme didn't work out, Domingo and Denver recorded 'Perhaps Love' as a duet, produced by Okun, who suggested to the two record companies that they co-release the collaboration as a single. This peace plan was scuppered by Weintraub, who wanted Domingo's management contract as part of the deal. Domingo was not looking to change his representation. They did, however, get to sing the song on an ABC network TV special, *20/20*.

The irony, of course, is that however reluctantly Denver went along with the 'fix' between RCA and Weintraub to send him down to Nashville, the results were by and large excellent. He was assigned to one of the top producers in town, Larry Butler, whose work with Kenny Rogers, just to take one example, transformed the former pop singer into a country legend who lies second only to Garth Brooks in the list of all-time greats, when judged on record sales. Denver, incidentally, the unwilling country star, weighs in at number seven on the same list, according to a 'Top Ten' documentary screened in the UK by Channel 4 in March 1999, where points were awarded for single and album sales to arrive at the overall chart.

The title song, 'Some Days Are Diamonds', by Dick Feller, is archetypal Denver material, where he finds that distinctive balance between purely-pitched singing and world-weary resignation that characterises some of his strongest work. And as Butler begins a slow fade out towards the end of the track Denver starts taking exhilarating liberties with the melody. As a single, the song reached the Top Ten of the country charts, and yet Denver dismissed the results as 'ersatz'.

'Country Love' was the follow-up, catchy and commercial, and now the new RCA regime began to look for a commitment to country music from Denver, so that they could slap a Nashville label on him, sweet-talk the influential country disc jockeys into accepting the singer as one of their own, and establish a fresh commercial niche for him. Denver refused to go along with them, and so they gave only lip service to promoting the record. It was now clear that the liaison between Denver and RCA could not survive – there was no meeting of minds. And since Jerry Weintraub had seen Nashville as a road to recovery for Denver, his interest too began to wane.

To cap a difficult period, the estrangement from Annie was now complete. Denver moved into their guest house, and began to spend more and more off-duty evenings in the local bar. In February 1981 the situation was formalised into an agreed six-month separation, and Denver took off on a visit to China and Tibet. By the autumn he was back in New York, recording the *Seasons of the Heart* album. He indulged in an affair, this time far more than a one-night stand, while working on the songs, and in November, symbolically, he lost his wedding ring while out boating. Annie's Christmas present, confirming that all was not lost, was a replacement, but Denver could not bring himself to wear it.

The album, released in the following February, was in some ways a diary of the break-up, or perhaps more precisely it had been a last-ditch scheme to prevent it. The title song, as personal as anything he ever wrote, keeps searching for reasons for reconciliation – they've always loved to go for walks together, for example, and 'I know we always will'. 'Are you trying to tell me something?' was Annie's quite reasonable, if cool, response.

And it is here that he gets his 'Perhaps Love' duet with Domingo on to vinyl at last, an exhaustive exploration of different aspects of the word 'love'. Erstwhile partner Barney Wyckoff co-produced the set with Denver himself, and this is a collection that the singer doubtless felt more at home with than the Nashville experiment. It was given a typically soft sound, but the heartfelt nature of the material prevented it from becoming too cloying. A song of separation, 'Shanghai Breezes', gave Denver his last pop entry in the Top 40.

It is ironic that, as his relationship with RCA was beginning to cool fast, his record company decided in 1981 to honour him with a special presentation. They had totted up the sums and realised that the *Greatest Hits* set from 1973 had now sold over ten million copies, the achievement that did more than anything else to lift Denver into that country-music pantheon mentioned above. RCA president Robert Summer said: 'John Denver is the first artist in the 80-year history of RCA Records to reach this sales plateau.' And he remains, of course, one of the very few to have achieved what in 1999 was to be officially dubbed by the record industry as a 'diamond' record, to go with his 14 golds and eight platinums. The Beatles will always have five such awards, and at the time that the idea of the diamond record was created, the phenomenal Garth Brooks was fast closing on them with four ten-million sellers.

Denver's father had left the air force in disillusion during the Vietnam War – though not, of course, over the righteousness of the conflict. Just the opposite, in fact. As the war deepened and more troops were needed, the authorities shortened the training time given to rookie pilots, a situation that, as a perfectionist teacher, he could not go along with. He then worked as a freight pilot for several years before, in the mid-'70s, Denver offered him a position as 'chief of Windstar Aviation'. In creating this role specifically for his father, Denver had ensured that they took one further step closer together. Henry John Sr stopped drinking, began to watch his diet and enjoyed his new role.

Early in 1982, however, he began to feel unwell. After attending a Denver show in Lake Tahoe he suffered a heart attack, at the age of 61, and was placed on a life-support machine in hospital. He was beyond recovery, however, and the lifeline was switched off on 15 March. This was to continue to be a traumatic year for Denver, since in the summer Annie sued for divorce. Their 15th wedding anniversary came and went uncelebrated on 9 June, the day after Denver had appeared at a concert for peace with Judy Collins and Jimmy Buffet.

That autumn, Denver was living in a lodge house belonging to him, once a 'family getaway', in Wood's Lake, a 90-minute drive from Aspen. Zak and Anna Kate were staying with him. On the drive out to the lake he had passed by the Snowmass home and had seen, to his outrage, that Annie had cut down a row of trees that to him was a vital component of the panorama as viewed from the front of the house. He armed himself with a power saw, symbolically reflecting what he saw as vandalism, and leaving the children with their nanny he drove back to Snowmass early one morning. He confronted Annie about the trees, and a furious argument developed. At one point he realised that he had his hands around her throat, and drew back in horror.

Instead of attacking her, he decided to leave a bizarre calling card. This must have been in his mind all along, since he had come prepared with the power saw. He started it up, and began by clipping a corner from the kitchen table. Then he cut clean through the dining table, and moving on to the bedroom he attacked the marital bed. The destruction continued until the bedsheets became entwined and choked the saw mechanism, bringing the rampage to a halt. The marriage was over.

These disruptions and crises in Denver's private life meant that recording was put on the back burner for a while. It was summer 1983 before he delivered another set to RCA, and it appeared in September, with Wyckoff still on board but Okun also re-appearing, sporting an 'executive producer' credit. There are some interesting ideas here – the bleakly pessimistic 'Falling Out of Love', for instance, is given a skipping, pitter-patter treatment that uses contrast to stress the lyric, bolstered by a sleazy saxophone part.

Denver's political side is catered for by the 'plea for understanding' meditation 'It's About Time', but the album's outstanding track is a vigorous duet with Emmylou Harris, 'Wild Montana Skies', in which Denver heads out for his beloved wide open spaces once again. He was choosing a strange way to stress his refusal to be identified as a country singer, crooning with the contemporary queen of the genre, urging the song along with Everly chords, and laying on dubs of banjo, steel, and fast-picked country Fender. As a single, it reached number 14 in the country list.

But no sooner was the album released than RCA rushed out another novelty item for the Christmas market, *Rocky Mountain Holiday,* which once again teamed Denver with The Muppets. This confusion of images – one that he wasn't particularly keen on, as a successful country singer and the other more familiar to the world at large, as a man who sings with cheeky dolls – could not have helped his career. Although Denver's record sales were never again to hit the peaks of the 1970s, however, his continued popularity as a live attraction was confirmed in 1984 when, at the St Louis VIP Fair, he played to three-quarters of a million people, the largest crowd he ever drew.

The relationship with Jerry Weintraub continued to decline, with Denver realising more and more that he was now simply a cog in the management machine, rather than the main driving force. The last straw came in autumn, 1984. Denver was committed to a European tour, playing solo, which without a band on the road would indeed have been a profitable venture. Weintraub, however, had set up a television movie project built around Denver's version of a Bobby Goldsboro song, 'The Cowboy and the Lady'. Expecting to go to work on it, Denver was forced to cancel the tour, only to find Weintraub putting the date for the film project back and back, while he concentrated his energies on another movie, another deal.

Once Denver realised that he had been left high and dry, double-whammied with no tour and no movie, he called the UK promoter and managed to reinstate the main British date, at the Royal Albert Hall. Because of his growing frustration with the situation back at home, both professional and personal, he recalled it as 'one of the most painful nights I've ever had working on a stage'. A few days of driving around Scotland, turning the problem over in his mind, resolved him to split with Weintraub. Denver returned to America for a confrontation, but Weintraub pointed out that there were three-and-a-half years left to run on the contract, and threatened to sue. He decided against going ahead with legal action, however, and Denver was a free man.

Another management experiment, handing his affairs over to two friends – his recent producer Barney Wyckoff and Don Coder – didn't work out either, and this time it did take a day in court to unravel the tie. It was clearly a civilised settlement, however, since Wyckoff was to be in attendance at Denver's memorial service in Aspen, giving testimony to how much the singer meant to his friends and fans.

In the meantime, Denver's relationship with RCA also

continued on a downward path. The cause of the rot dated back to 1981, when they had turned down 'Perhaps Love', insisted on him cutting the Nashville album with Weintraub's agreement and then failed to promote it. RCA was bought out by General Electric, a company heavily involved, apart from anything else, in the armaments industry. They could not have one of their major acts singing at peace concerts and visiting Eastern Europe and China. By the time they, in turn, sold on the company to the Bartlesmann Music Group (BMG) they had, in Denver's words, 'become an organisation of pure opportunists', and it was time to get out.

In November 1984 there was yet another *Greatest Hits* compilation, this time trawling back as far as the *I Want to Live* set, by which time Denver was working with a new producer, Roger Nichols, on the next set. Nichols was perhaps best-known at the time for his work with Steely Dan. He edged Denver towards a distinctly different sound, moving into the soft-rock mainstream where a polite version of Philly soul meets cabaret rock. The title track, 'Dreamland Express', was to prove the only commercial success of any note, ironically edging into the country Top Ten – Denver had established a market among country fans in spite of himself, and though there was nothing discernibly 'country' about this straightforward pop song, his appeal lingered after the notable success with Emmylou Harris.

More indicative of the change in direction were the slinky, tongue-in-cheek doo-wop pastiche 'I'm in the Mood to be Desired Tonight' and the sensuous 'Don't Close Your Eyes Tonight'. There was little of the 'real' Denver in either song, but he was professional enough to adopt the required personae with conviction. Closer to his heart was 'African Sunrise', a direct result of his first visit to the continent as part of a fact-finding delegation on behalf of the Hunger Project. On *Portrait* Denver referred to the promotional video made for 'Don't Close Your Eyes Tonight' as 'the first real modern video I did,' although he

142

pointed out that he had previously been a pioneer in the use of film segments to illustrate songs at live concerts.

He was engagingly modest in his assessment of the video: 'This had a little bit of an acting opportunity in it, and it tried to tell a little bit of a story, and it gave me the opportunity if not to be a little bit sexy at least to be in a sexy kind of role, which I enjoyed enormously.' Looking at this quote – and I have tidied it up somewhat – it is striking that Denver/Deutschendorf did seem to have a habit in interviews of speaking English as a second language, as if in this case he had just lit upon the phrase 'a little bit'.

The video also confirmed to the general television audience that Denver now had an image far from that of the pebble glasses and face-splitting grin. Here he moved from blue-collar work clothes to smooth evening dress, he used no obvious aids to vision, and his role was indeed 'a little bit sexy'. *Dreamland Express* was to take Denver into the album chart for the last time under RCA's colours, but indicative of his dwindling mass appeal was the fact that it peaked at number 90.

Denver was always keen on 'acting opportunities', and this could well have proved a signpost towards the future had he lived. His best piece of work, he felt, was in a made-for-television movie when he was teamed with those great veterans Hume Cronyn and Jessica Tandy in a drama called *Foxfire*. He referred to his co-stars as 'those two masters of American theatre . . . I could never express how much I learned just being around them and watching them work'.

In 1985 Denver was in Japan, performing at a benefit concert intended to promote a conference on freshwater pollution. As someone who had spent so many years campaigning for a whole raft of causes that included world hunger, through his Hunger Project, and who for the last 20 years of his life worked selflessly for UNICEF, Denver was undoubtedly hurt that no telephone call came from Bob Geldof in the late spring of the year, when

Geldof was busy setting up the mammoth Live Aid spectacular. Denver's devotion to the cause, it would seem, could not outweigh his terminal unhipness, and so the opportunity to earn world-wide Brownie points, in front of the biggest television audience in history, went to such tireless activists for an end to world hunger as Status Quo.

As a means of publicising the desperate ravages of famine, as a fundraising and consciousness-raising exercise and simply as an exhilarating concert, Live Aid was, of course, a huge success. But one cannot help feeling that, when it comes to a pop star with a long-term knowledge of the problem, John Denver and not Bob Geldof was the acknowledged expert. He should have been invited, and he would undoubtedly have had only the charitable object, and not global publicity, in mind. And surely a rousing chorus of 'Country Roads' could not have spoiled the atmosphere – after all, the biggest coup of the event was scored by Phil Collins who, thanks to Concorde, performed in both London and Philadelphia. Surely no one else could have been accused of driving in the middle of the road when Collins was so centrally involved. And hadn't George Michael just quit a teenybop duo with a school chum who couldn't sing and whose guitar was never plugged in?

In the autumn of 1985 Denver visited the Soviet Union. Cultural ties between America and the Soviet bloc had been severed in 1980, and the Moscow Olympics held in that year had been boycotted, in protest at the Soviet invasion of Afghanistan, and so for Denver to visit the country and perform had taken nearly a year to set up. He was there in the autumn to promote his forthcoming tour, and to finalise arrangements.

In Leningrad he was taken to the Piskaryovka Cemetery, where 470,000 victims of the 900-day siege of Leningrad were buried, in mass graves denoting simply the year of death. By mid-1941 the German army had conquered Latvia, Lithuania, Belorussia and most of the Ukraine, and laid siege to Leningrad

144

in August. The brave resistance of the city, decimated by starvation, continued until the Red Army liberated it in January 1944, by which time the tide of the war was on the turn.

Denver was inspired by his grim sightseeing trip to write 'Let Us Begin', another of his passionate polemics whose subject matter is indicated by its subtitle, 'What Are We Making Weapons For?' Again, this was not a sentiment likely to endear Denver to General Electric – in fact it was probably the last straw in the declining relationship between the record company and the man who for so long had been their biggest star.

And so, when he returned to the Soviet Union in the spring of 1986 for his concert tour, RCA ignored this ground-breaking venture even though he was still under contract to them. The tour was sponsored by Pepsico, but Denver was later to calculate that without record-company support he lost half-a-million dollars by going.

On his first trip he had been introduced to a Soviet counterpart, the singer Alexander Gradsky, known as Sacha, and they recorded the song together when Denver returned – later still they duetted on television by satellite, with Denver back home in America and Gradsky in Moscow. The record also included the Red Army Chorus. For the promotional video, Denver's friend Obie Benz assembled a telling sequence of archive images to support Denver's pacifist lyric, and the singer was later to call the song 'simply the best piece of work that I've done in my career'.

From Russia the intrepid Denver went on to China, for negotiations in Beijing about a possible satellite TV special, but he and Hal Thau could not agree terms with the intransigent Chinese television network. In 1992, however, Denver's persistence paid off, and he became the first western artist to tour China.

In June 1986 Denver's last RCA album, *One World*, was released, with Roger Nichols once again producing. It included a two-year-old track in which he duetted with the French pop singer Sylvie Vartan, a pleasant-enough ballad called 'Love Again' which crept into the lower reaches of the Hot Hundred, as well as 'Let Us Begin'. Overall, this was a more personal set than its predecessor, exemplified by its stand-out track, 'Flying For Me', Denver's deeply-felt response to the Challenger tragedy.

It was well known – and for some it was a source of considerable hilarity – that Denver had developed a burning ambition to be the first civilian in space, and at one stage even offered the Russians money, reputedly $10 million, to be sent up to the Mir space station and sing down to the world. He became active in the Citizen in Space programme partly in the hope of furthering his ambitions, although more altruistically because of 'a very positive feeling about what we can learn about ourselves and our beautiful blue Earth here floating in space'. He underwent the NASA induction programme and succeeded in reaching the shortlist.

In fact, the tragic honour fell to a school teacher from Concord, New Hampshire, Christa McAuliffe. She was one of seven astronauts who boarded the space shuttle Challenger on 28 January 1986, taking off from Cape Canaveral at 11.38 a.m. The world watched as, 73 seconds into what had looked like a perfect lift-off, one of the liquid hydrogen tanks exploded, seemingly caused by a faulty seal on one of the booster rockets. McAuliffe died along with Commander Michael J. Smith and the rest of his crew.

'I was making a film in Georgetown, Colorado,' recalled Denver, 'and didn't know that the accident had occurred. My son Zak called me . . . As I sat and watched the news that evening, as usually happens in times of great emotional distress I found my guitar in my hands, and I was playing kind of a meditation as I watched what was going on.'

'Flying For Me' was one of Denver's finest songs, born out of that grim experience. Maybe, in view of that uncanny interview given just before he died when he expressed a wish to die in flight, he 'should have been on that plane', just as bass-player Waylon Jennings should have died with his employer, Buddy Holly. The video Denver made to promote the song ended with a tribute to the Challenger crew and showed the blast-off from Canaveral. But instead of following the space craft skywards towards that all-too-familiar and grotesquely beautiful starburst explosion, he chose the telling shot from the camera that remained earthbound, capturing the gradually-spreading billow of smoke from around the take-off gantry, slowly filling the screen while the rocket sped towards oblivion.

After the *One World* album it was clear that RCA no longer really had any interest in Denver at all. Maybe the time for his music, uncompromising as he was, had passed anyway, but he also identified a general decline in business morality in the country at large that was at odds with his campaigning spirit. After all, the causes he adopted were inevitably in opposition to the amoral conduct of business – peace could not co-exist with the multi-billion dollar armaments trade, and the wilderness could not be left in the hands of the land-rapists eager to consume its mineral wealth. Denver identified the new morality, based on the concept of 'looking after number one', squarely with President Ronald Reagan.

This destructive philosophy found its exact mirror image in Britain, where Reagan's soulmate, Margaret Thatcher, was busily destroying the pit-props of basic decent behaviour that had until then informed the conduct of the country. Those who worked in the manufacturing industry, who actually made things of use to the community, were treated with contempt, largely because of their habit of huddling together in bolshy trade unions for protection.

Not only was profit now the only God in both the US and the UK, but it was defined in its narrowest sense. Each industry, each factory, had to stand on its own financial feet. Reaganomics and

147

Thatcherism were founded upon the crudest of economic theories, and took no account of the domino effect of such simplistic mathematics – the business dies, its suppliers die, unemployment spreads outwards, the local carpet companies and the white goods manufacturers and the estate agents and the travel companies and the corner garage have no customers, the local economy spirals downwards until it stagnates, and another area of the country is given over to hopeless blight and the drugged despair of poverty. Neither Reagan nor Thatcher were too bothered about the 'scorched earth' effects of their policies.

The new heroes were now to be found on Wall Street and in the City of London, making personal fortunes by gambling on how much further, for example, the third-world producers of coffee could be exploited. A singer of simple love songs, of the celebration of nature, a preacher of the immorality of conflict and the urgent need for conservation, was out of kilter with such bleakly callous times. And there seems to be no irony in the fact that Denver was a multi-millionaire. He had always followed the most naïve and honest of career plans – to write songs that he liked and hope that enough people agreed with him. Millions did, and so by and large he never had to compromise.

FOURTEEN

The Last Decade

In the spring of 1986, before the release of *One World*, Denver went over to Australia for a tour. His popularity there had always remained very strong. Almost constant touring was becoming necessary, not only in an attempt to prevent record sales from dwindling further but also because the Windstar Foundation remained a permanent drain on Denver's pocket. It was never designed, of course, to be a profit-making concern, but it would have taken far more assiduous stewardship than he could offer to prevent the losses from mounting. As Carrie Click, who worked for Denver back in Aspen, said after the singer's death, 'It started as a dream of his, but in the late '80s, when it was floundering, he was writing a very substantial cheque every single month to keep it afloat.' And in the month before his death Denver was to say of Windstar: 'It is one of the things that I'm most proud of in my life.'

The down-under tour finished up in Sydney, where he was also booked to take part in the televised 'Loggies' Awards show. This annual bash recognised achievements in music, television and film in Australia, and Denver had been invited to perform a song and present the Show of the Year award. In the hotel bar before the event he spotted a woman wearing a white dress, who turned out to be a 26-year-old Australian singer called Cassandra Delaney. He later discovered this because she had also seen him, and made contact. After what must qualify as a 'whirlwind

149

romance', Cassandra left her boyfriend for Denver, some 18 years her senior, and made the instant decision to travel with him to America. She had not even taken the trouble to apply for a visa, but thanks to Denver's celebrity this was accepted as an oversight, and she was allowed entry to the US.

A week later they left once more for a European tour, something that few Americans were doing at the time. The previous June, Arab terrorists had hijacked a TWA airliner and taken 39 American hostages, who were held for 17 days in Beirut before a successful operation to free them was carried out. Potential American tourists regarded the choice of a cruise holiday as similarly risky, with memories of the seizing of the *Achille Lauro* fresh in their minds – in that case the terrorists had cold-bloodedly murdered a disabled American by shooting him and then tipping him overboard. And then, on 16 April 1986, US warplanes attacked Tripoli in retaliation for Libyan involvement in the bombing of a West Berlin discotheque, which had been popular with off-duty American servicemen. Undaunted, Denver headed for Berlin. The UK was included on the itinerary, as always, and during his concert at the Liverpool Empire 'Mother Nature's son' ad-libbed a 15-minute Beatles medley.

Back home, he remained one of the most popular stars on network television. He broadcast seasonal shows from different parts of the country, each with the flavour of the state he was in. His Christmas show of 1987 reunited him with The Muppets and also starred Julie Andrews, and he was later summoned to Washington to record a one-off special in front of President Bush, called *In Performance at the White House.*

Two years after their meeting, Denver and Cassie were back in Sydney, and they were married on 12 August 1988. Although Denver had until then resigned himself to never become a natural father, due to a low sperm count, recent advances in treatment had given him new hope. After a further visit to the

Soviet Union – it was at this point that he tried to achieve his bizarre ambition of being flown to the Mir space station to perform for the whole world – Cassie was confirmed as being pregnant.

That winter, and into the spring of 1989, the couple stayed at home in Aspen, and their daughter Jesse Belle was born. 'For a little while,' recalled Denver, 'Cassandra and I reconstituted paradise.' Soon, however, tensions began to surface once again in Denver's doomed private life. Cassie was not a stay-at-home type – certainly not in Aspen, which she quite understandably identified with Denver's first marriage – and was also eager to resume her career in Australia. In the meantime Denver was locked in a dispute with Annie over whether they should sell the first marital home, the dream house Denver had helped to design.

One night, performing in Dublin, Denver realised that whenever the word 'home' cropped up in a song he immediately saw that house in Starwood in his imagination, which confirmed to him that this was indeed the 'home' he had never known as a child. It made him determined to hang on to the house at all costs, but Cassie was ever more insistent on leaving Aspen for Australia. It was an insoluble dilemma, and not one that could possibly allow for a successful marriage. They stayed in Aspen at his insistence, and grew further and further apart. To the torment Denver was feeling at having seemingly failed at marriage for a second time was added humiliation, as Cassie made no attempt to hide her local infidelities. Denver sued for divorce, and Cassie moved to Los Angeles with Jesse Belle.

The night after the final hearing of the divorce, on 21 August 1993, Denver drank too much at the local bar and was, as he quaintly put it, 'stopped by the local constabulary' when attempting to drive home. A brief driving ban and a community service order resulted, and he fulfilled it in part by performing a benefit concert for the local sheriff's Tipsy Taxi service, which was organised in order to get drunks home safely.

During the years of his second marriage Denver continued to record, distributing the product through his own Windstar Records. The first, *Higher Ground*, appeared in September 1989 and the title song tied in with a television movie of the same name that Denver had made in the previous year, the pilot show for a hoped-for series. It was set in Alaska, a vast corner of the USA whose threatened ecology was to become a campaigning cause for Denver, and he played a pilot called Jim Clayton.

Later in the year he put out another of his seasonal collections, *Christmas Like a Lullaby*, cut in Nashville with his remarkable roster of musicians – Glen D. Hardin and James Burton were joined by bassist Jerry Scheff, drummer Jerry Carrigan, Jim Horn on brass and woodwind, and percussionist Machito Sanchez. It was another smooth mix of the sacred and secular, and included a return to Tom Paxton's 'The Marvellous Toy'.

In 1989 Denver also collaborated with the Nitty Gritty Dirt Band, who returned to the idea they had first put into practise in 1972, *Will the Circle Be Unbroken?* This was a panorama of country involving some of the biggest names in the genre spread over three albums, and the guest artists first time round included Roy Acuff, Merle Travis, Doc Watson, Maybelle Carter and Earl Scruggs. The second set, 17 years later, called on more contemporary partners like Emmylou Harris, Roger McGuinn and John Prine. Denver's track with the band, 'And So It Goes', made inroads into the country chart, and the project won the 1989 Album of the Year award from the Country Music Association.

In 1990 came a couple of albums that duplicated some songs, *Earth Songs* and *The Flower that Shattered the Stone*. The latter was undoubtedly the strongest set from this last decade of Denver's career, and it even reintroduced him briefly to the charts – although you would have had to scan down as far as the 185th slot to spot it, and this would have meant little in terms of actual sales. The title track is a stately meditation written by

Denver's sometime collaborators Joe Henry and John Jarvis, which Denver later re-cut as a duet with the Japanese singer Kosetsu Minami.

Another outstanding track, 'Eagles and Horses', inevitably recalls the pantheism and vocal pyrotechnics of 'The Eagle and the Hawk' in its celebration of natural power. A song inspired by the *Exxon Valdez* disaster, 'Raven's Child', is discussed below, while the set's other highlight, 'Postcard from Paris', was referred to by Denver on the *Portrait* video.

It was written by Jimmy Webb who, beginning in the late 1960s, wrote a string of hits using a map of America as his inspiration – 'By the Time I Get to Phoenix', 'Wichita Lineman', 'Galveston' and the bizarre, over-the-top epic for Richard Harris, 'MacArthur Park', which enough people took seriously to escort it to the top of the charts. 'Postcard from Paris' stretched his geographical boundaries a little further, and Denver understood Webb to have written it specifically with him in mind. Webb played piano on the session, and Denver amusingly recalled his chain-smoking habit. 'He would sit there playing the piano each take that we did, and as he did this little arpeggio at the end he'd hit that last note and reach up and grab the cigarette while he was still sustaining the note . . .'

When Denver came to make a video to promote the single release of 'Postcard' he related the images specifically to the Gulf War, beginning and ending with shots of a soldier writing home, though of course this topical connection was not explicit in the writing. The war had broken out in August, just before the release of the album, and had been prompted by the Iraqi invasion of Kuwait, which threatened the West's oil supplies. The West's reason for going to war, however, was apparently not to protect its oil but more grandly 'to restore democracy to Kuwait', which rather overlooks the fact that something can only be restored if it exists in the first place. Denver's video made an effective link between the lyric and the brief and distant war

153

being fought out on the television screens all over America, depicting a soldier in the Gulf wishing 'he could be anywhere but where he is'.

A year after *The Flower that Shattered the Stone* came another Windstar set, *Different Directions*, with a song suite from his television movie *Foxfire* and more songs exploring Denver's two, related concerns – the glories of the natural world, and the threats to it brought about by greed and exploitation. The message was becoming more relevant by the day, but as a commercial proposition in the record market it was clear that Denver's own day had passed. His living now came from television and from touring, usually as a portable solo act like in his earliest days, sometimes spiked with a rhythm section or a guest guitarist, or with pre-recorded tapes for some of the songs.

Although he was fading from the charts, as a performer, as a celebrity, as a campaigner, Denver retained his extraordinary popularity and fame, and he noted with some awe on the *Portrait* commentary that it transcended national boundaries and age groups. 'To go to a commune in China, to go to a village in Africa, to be in . . . the largest slum in the world on the outskirts of Bombay . . . and have little kids running after you saying, "John Denver, John Denver, sing 'Country Roads'" . . . how does something like that happen?' In 1992, Denver became the first Western artist to tour China, and in 1994 he also became the first American performer to visit Vietnam after the war, which had ended in 1975. As with his work in the Soviet Union, which had included a big benefit concert for the victims of the Chernobyl disaster, he was articulating a protest against Cold War divisiveness. This was recognised in 1993 with the award of the Albert Schweitzer Music Prize, which is given for outstanding humanitarian achievements.

In 1995 Denver performed in New York at the Wildlife Concert, and his act, drawn mainly from his 'greatest hits', was released on a double CD. Later, a package of conventional CD and CD-ROM, using material filmed at the Wildlife Concert, was also put out, and included clips of Denver in performance.

In August 1995 Denver was introduced to his page on the World Wide Web for the first time, prior to going 'online' to answer questions from fans. Needless to say he was not subjected to a merciless grilling and Denver could, by and large, fall back on comforting clichés. Yes, he was very much looking forward to playing in your town, he enjoyed all sorts of music, and his favourite song was usually the most recent one he'd written.

No, he did not think that hunters should be allowed to use electronic devices to assist them in killing cougars. He adroitly avoided the invitation to condemn 'MTV grunge-rock' by saying, 'I really don't watch MTV,' but he did reveal that not much modern country music appealed to him. This, of course, had become a sore point since the days when RCA had tried to turn him into an out-and-out country singer, and his stubborn attitude had undoubtedly been detrimental to his career, since the country chart was now the one most likely to sport his name.

On the Web, Denver identified his first composition as the effort of a 13-year-old, 'Lazy Little Stream', confirming that 'from the very beginning, nature was a part of my self-expression'. He gave a convincing, well-prepared message about each individual's contribution towards creating a better environment. 'There are so many things that need to be done that sometimes it seems overwhelming. I try to remind everyone that no one person has to do it all, but if each one of us follows our heart and our own inclinations we will find the small things we can do and together we will come up with enough to create a sustainable future and a healthy environment.'

His most interesting comment edged towards a personal definition of pantheism, in the accessible form that I have chosen to refer to as a recurrent motif in this book. 'It's so important that we always remember that nature, environment, wild places and wild things are a big part of what makes us who and what we are as human beings. To deny this is to deny our own heritage, our own spirit and our own souls. We must learn to live in a sustainable fashion in a way that promotes the incredible diversity of life in this world rather than decreasing it mindlessly. We must not allow people to destroy those things [that] are so precious and cannot be replaced.'

What I take from this is Denver's understanding that in seeking our spiritual nourishment we are interdependent with the rest of the natural world. This is a vital element in the concept that God exists in all things, and all things are part of God. And what Denver is trying to make clear is that we are all – environmentalists and oil barons, atheists and believers – dependent on this harmonious balance between man and the natural world. In the end, to extend this argument, naked self-interest should demand that we are environmentally aware.

In the last years of his life, RCA showed a reawakened interest in re-promoting Denver's past glories, and a number of compilations appeared in the USA, Australia and the UK, forcing the big record stores to remake a 'John Denver' divider card for their display racks. In 1996 RCA assembled a handsome double CD containing 39 tracks drawn from Denver's entire career on the label, called *The Rocky Mountain Collection*. It was widely promoted, put at the top of the country-music list by influential Tower Records, and it sold well.

In the following year they released an even more ambitious anthology, this time in the Digipak format which allows four CDs to be packaged as a hardback book, with far greater scope for text and artwork than is possible inside a conventional plastic CD container, and less wear and tear on the fingernails. *The Country Roads Collection*, all 79 tracks of it, was alas to become a memorial to Denver's career. At the time of his death yet another compilation, *The Best of John Denver Live*, had restored him to the country charts as well. A further collection released after his death saw him return to Nashville, in 1996, for a self-produced, acoustic, solo revisit to 16 of his songs. In the UK it was licensed from Windstar by EMI, who dubbed it *The Unplugged Collection.*

In the spring of 1997, on the back of excellent reviews for *The Rocky Mountain Collection,* Denver returned to the UK for an extensive tour. He was a solo act now, using backing tapes where he wanted a thickening of the sound, and he seemed in excellent spirits. He also seemed to have turned the corner in his on-off fight to prevent alcohol taking over his life. He proved that he had lost nothing of the skill that was always at the heart of his popularity as a concert performer – of turning a vast venue into a front-room hoedown.

There was a crowd of 5,000, for example, at The Point in Dublin, where he played on 23 March. As reported by Tom Gilmore in *Country Music People,* he introduced 'Take Me Home, Country Roads' as a song he had performed on Chinese television. 'I'm told China has over 700 million people,' he said, 'so all I need is for every fourth or fifth person there to buy my next album.' Of 'Mother Nature's Son', the song that could have been written about him, he referred to Paul McCartney and said, 'I don't know how he got it first.' His new-found enthusiasm for golf was reflected in a rewrite of Tennessee Ernie Ford's '16 Tons' as '18 Holes', and he indulged in country comedy with such songs as 'Get Your Tongue Out of My Mouth, I'm Kissing You Goodbye'. A buoyant, good-humoured Denver pulling in the fans by the thousand, and a 'best of' record in the charts – what was that about a slump in his career?

Meanwhile, Denver remained as active as ever in his extra-musical life. The ecological threat to Alaska, the 49th state of the Union, was typical of Denver's concerns outside music, and in 1996 he published a brief manifesto called *Alaska: a Challenge for Democracy.* This was very much a return to the theme for him, as in 1979 he had made a television documentary, *Alaska: America's Child,* developing his thesis that the environmental mistakes that had been made during the course of 200 years in the 'lower 48' states were about to be repeated, but this time in a far shorter and therefore even more disastrous time-scale. The film, produced by John Wilcox for ABC, was instrumental in increasing the lobby from ecology organisations in favour of the Alaskan Land Bill, which aimed to set aside protected land that could not be violated by the pyramid of business interests supporting the mining and logging industries.

Alaska is the largest peninsula in the western hemisphere, over 590,000 square miles in area, and the conflict between development and conservation has been a long-running and sometimes bitter one. The first oil and natural gas discoveries were made in the 1950s in the south, on the Kenai Peninsula just below Anchorage, and within 20 years these had developed into the most important of the state's mineral industries. To such an isolated and often barren land, the further discovery in 1968 of petroleum deposits in the north, on the coast of the Arctic Ocean, promised an economic boom, but first the problems of transporting the oil across the vast state and on down to the lower 48 had to be resolved. In spite of an income to Alaska of $1 billion derived from petrol company revenue in the following year, the proposal to build a pipeline running almost due south to the sheltered harbour of Valdez remained hugely controversial.

In November 1973 the US Congress passed a bill that made the construction possible, and work began in the following year. In June 1979 the pipeline, nearly 800 miles long, pumped its first oil from the Prudhoe Bay field, way up in the Arctic Circle. Between Valdez and the Gulf of Alaska, gateway to the southern market, lies Prince William Sound, and it was here on 24 March 1989 that the environmental cost of this industry was dramatically and tragically illustrated, when the supertanker *Exxon Valdez*, almost 1,000 feet long, ran aground on Bligh Reef soon after leaving Valdez and caused the most disastrous oil spill in American – and possibly world – history. The long-term consequences of such a disaster to the environment and to the balance of marine ecology could not, of course, be stated as fact at the time, only guessed at – whether by pessimistic environmental activists or optimistic industry apologists.

John Denver was undeniably an activist, though he retained his optimism. He stood beside Jimmy Carter when the President signed the Alaska Land Conservation Act, itself a compromise, decreeing that 15 per cent of Alaska's land mass, including 125 miles of shoreline, was so precious as an unspoilt natural resource that no amount of potential mineral wealth could justify its desecration. Just 15 per cent seemed like a victory against the all-powerful forces of economic exploitation.

Ten years on from the *Exxon Valdez* oil spill, continuous research into the disaster revealed that the pessimists were correct. The studies were published as a paper in *Environmental Toxicology and Chemistry*, picked up by *Scientific American* among other journals, and reported in *The Observer* of 7 March 1999. Fish with incomplete tails, twisted backbones and inflated stomachs were still being caught in Prince William Sound, and it was estimated that an oil concentration of less than one part per billion would kill marine life.

Dr Bruce Wright of the US National Maritime Fisheries Service in Alaska said chillingly that 'even rain falling on car parks will flush oil that has leaked from engines and carry it into drains and then into streams and bays. Marine life will be killed off even if only tiny traces of oil are present.'

The trace of oil from the *Exxon Valdez* amounted to 11 million gallons. As the years of research progressed, one finding was that the heavier elements in crude oil – once thought to be comparatively inert and therefore less harmful than more volatile components – were in fact the real problem, remaining in the water in the long term and releasing their minute, fatal doses.

When the tenth anniversary of the disaster arrived, however, the Exxon corporation was still contesting a $5.4 billion judgement against it, delivered seven years previously, and had agreed only to smaller payouts in compensation. It took that long, for instance, for the Eyak Indians in the fishing town worst affected, Cordova, to receive a mere $18,000 each, the first instalment of a payout to compensate for the destruction of their livelihood. An Exxon employee, Frank Sprow, grandly named vice-president for environment and safety, claimed, as quoted in *The Times* of 25 March 1999: 'The Sound is healthy, robust and thriving. Mother Nature, if you will, has remarkable powers of recovery.' Many a twisted, two-headed fish disagreed.

The *Exxon Valdez* disaster inspired one of Denver's most impressive environmental songs, 'Raven's Child', included on *Earth Songs* and also on the next Windstar album, *The Flower that Shattered the Stone*. On the *Portrait* video he explained: 'If, as an environmentalist, we're against anything then I would say we are against the arrogance of power and the most obscene way it shows up, which is greed.' He visited Prince William Sound in the grim aftermath of the disaster. By then the oil slick stretched for 500 miles. It had already blackened hundreds of miles of coast, and the slaughter among seabirds and fish was incalculable. Denver saw a boat called *Raven's Child*, 'seemingly trying to wash the oil slick off the top of the water . . .' This inspired a far more wide-ranging meditation on that arrogance and greed he referred to, although as he pointed out: '. . . As always I try to turn it around to a very positive feeling . . .'

The video assembled from archive footage and newsreels to accompany this song, beginning among the crack houses on the 'streets of despair', moving through Reagan's 'Star Wars' fantasy and cataloguing a string of examples of how the abuse of power results in horrific cruelty, before moving gradually towards hope – the defiance of the lone student in Tiananmen Square, the fall of the Berlin Wall, the release of Nelson Mandela – is surely one of the most uncompromising music promotion tools ever made. The world of the music video is usually one where narcissism and half-baked surrealism fight for attention. Few objective observers might have predicted that it would be John Denver, the grinning cowboy, who would turn the form into such effective agitprop.

To return to his *Challenge for Democracy*, he wrote it because the decision to preserve a proportion of Alaska as a wilderness seemed threatened by subsequent Congress resolutions. These would allow petroleum and gas exploration, and hence extraction, from what should have been protected land within the Arctic National Wildlife Refuge. Had America, Denver asked rhetorically, exhausted Prudhoe Bay? The answer was negative – indeed, improvements in extraction technology had extended the life of its reserves. Nor had territory already deemed available for drilling been fully explored as yet.

Denver blamed central government for the risk to the environment. And this, of course, was no longer the government of the half-witted war-mongerer Ronald Reagan, one of whose officials had famously shrugged off American connivance at torture and murder in South America with the memorable phrase, 'They're only little brown people.' This was the administration of Bill Clinton, who may have had lifelong trouble with his trousers but as a supposed liberal should surely have known better when it came to environmental desecration – in spite of his past forays into the murky realms of land speculation.

Denver urged American citizens to protest to their political representatives, to ensure continued protection not just of the Arctic National Wildlife Refuge but of other surviving wilderness areas – he gave the Red Rocks Wilderness in Utah as an example – against gas and oil development. He stressed of the proposed legislation: 'It is not needed and it is not wanted.' And he went on to point out that greater efficiency in using existing resources, and better conservation practices, was a more businesslike approach in any case, when compared to more and more costly exploration of more and more as-yet unravished places.

In a telling phrase, Denver widened his attack when asking who the government actually represented. Was it, he asked, 'the American people or the special interest groups like the oil companies, the tobacco companies, the National Rifle Association and others who can buy the legislators . . . with lobbying dollars?'. Violation of the countryside, after all, was always carried out to profit the few, not the many. 'To be human is to be nourished by the wild country,' argued Denver, and simply to know that the mountain eagle, the grizzly bear and the caribou could continue to live on unviolated land uplifted one's spirit.

These are not the sentiments one might immediately associate with a jet-flying American in a cowboy hat and a lumber jacket, but then, as we know, Denver cut through so many stereotypes.

The importance of concern for the environment, typified by his activities in the field of conservation, was chillingly emphasised in a report published by the World Wide Fund for Nature a year after Denver's death. The WWF launched its Living Planet Index, the most ambitious and far-reaching attempt yet to chart the threat to the natural world and its resources. The Index is a continuous record analogous to those that chart overall stock market changes. It draws on available data concerning population declines in animal and plant species, taking 1970 as its baseline with a notional index value of 100. By 1995 the Index stood at 68 and was still falling. In other words it could be argued that one third of the natural world had been destroyed in a quarter of a century.

'It is safe to say that the period since 1970 has been the most destructive in the history of the natural world since the great extinction 65 million years ago, when the meteor hit the Caribbean and wiped out the dinosaurs,' said the deputy director of WWF International, Jorgen Randers, as reported in *The Independent* of 2 October 1998.

In some vital areas, such as tropical rainforests, no one doubted that the percentage decline in terms of acreage was even greater, and that the fauna ecosystem of such environments could have been doubly affected. The elegantly named Sir Ghillean Prance, of the Royal Botanic Gardens in Kew, west London, put the rainforest shrinkage during this period at nearly one half. In fact, forests overall have declined in area far less dramatically, around 10 per cent, thanks to deliberate reafforestation – the 'sustainable resources' that so many commercial companies now realise furnish them with a potent and acceptable slogan. However, as anyone who has walked through a silent, seemingly lifeless and strictly regimented conifer plantation will confirm, simply replanting commercially useful trees does not necessarily support a thriving animal population – their needs and those of the timber trade do not coincide.

The WWF Index is matched by another measure, that of the pressures on the environment caused by human consumption, the direct cause of the threat to other life on the planet. This produces another frightening figure – if demand was 100 in 1970, by 1995 it was 163. As the WWF inputs more and more data into its computerised global watch, narrowing its admitted margin of possible error below the current 10–15 per cent, it will publish increasingly accurate figures on an annual basis. What it needs, of course, is a John Denver eager to use his celebrity to publicise such an urgent cause.

In the summer of 1997 Denver's name appeared in the ultra-trendy British men's magazine *FHM*. It reported on a survey of the most popular in-car songs, the ones you can sing along to while driving alone without anyone knowing your guilty secret. At the very top of the list was 'Take Me Home, Country Roads', brushing off such contenders as Van Morrison's 'Brown-Eyed Girl' and Don MacLean's 'American Pie'. It was an honour, of a sort. Denver had clearly been aware of the poll during his tour a couple of months earlier, referring to himself as a traffic-jam favourite.

Indeed, there were signs towards the end of his life of some sort of rehabilitation of his reputation. Part tongue-in-cheek, part genuine, it seemed similar in retrospect to the ABBA revival of 1999. Denver himself was aware, for example, of an album called *Heavy Denver*, on which 'these guys all wore little round glasses and overalls without T-shirts. It was a punk rock band and they played the hell out of those songs'. And there was another tribute album called *Minneapolis Does Denver*, on which various artists sang their favourite Denver tunes. Meanwhile Jason and the Scorchers had revived 'Take Me Home, Country Roads', and 'Rocky Mountain High' was used on a television beer commercial.

The last album Denver recorded, appeared on the Sony label, just before his death, a collection of train songs called *All Aboard*. The romance of the railroad, of course, runs deep in American culture, dating from the days when the pioneering engineers gradually opened up the continent and eventually linked the established cities of the east to the newly-charted west. Add to this Denver's fascination with transport – though more of the Porsche and Lear Jet variety – and it is perhaps surprising that he had not already delved into this treasury of material, except for occasional items in his repertoire like Steve Goodman's 'City of New Orleans', which was reprised here. The CD includes a 'secret' track not listed on the packaging, a song for his natural daughter Jesse Belle.

Denver also retained a huge and loyal hardcore fan base, in spite of the overall decline in his career. There can be little doubt that, had he been willing to make that all-important 'commitment' to country music, he had the innate talent to re-establish himself as a Nashville artist. Many of his biggest songs had brought out the country side of his music, and the album he had recorded there in 1981, 'under protest', was a far greater artistic success than he was willing to admit.

But he refused the commitment, partly, no doubt, out of cussedness and a dislike of the way he was being coerced in a particular direction by people he didn't trust, but also surely because he had done it all once already. He had reached higher in the music business than almost anyone else, and yet he knew that he had still failed to balance stardom and domestic contentment. On the other hand, he was left with quite enough money to allow him to spend his days on the golf course, his new obsession, and in pursuing his love of small planes. And so, on the last day of his life, that's exactly what he chose to do.

In Memoriam

Reading through the tributes of fans both before and after John Denver's death, expressing what his music meant to them, one is first struck by a uniformity in the choice of words. It is almost eerie, as if this was the prescribed mode of speech employed by some happy cult, the Denver Moonies. But this immediate impression is perhaps unworthy, since there is nothing whatsoever sinister in Denver's work – on the contrary, it is the goddammed wholesomeness that seems to be the uniting factor.

One of his admirers wishes 'there was some way I could thank you for the gift of beautiful music you have brought the world'. This is typical of the allegiance that Denver inspired. When a businessman sells you something, as Denver sold his records, you do not usually thank him as if it was a gift. The fan celebrates the fact that the songs 'have caused me to be thoughtful, at peace, motivated, consoled, inspired, introspective, renewed and so on'. This is sincerely and delicately expressed, and hints at the remarkable healing power of pop music.

What is unusual is that these are clearly the words of a mature and intelligent being. The ability of pop icons to take over the souls of their adherents is normally given only to hyped teenyboppers with a limited shelf life, obeying the built-in obsolescence of the music industry. An extension of this, reaching into the confused, doomy late teens, is the effect of such narcissistic melancholics as Richey Edwards, who performed a mysterious disappearance from the Manic Street Preachers, or Morrissey of The Smiths. Such performers know, either intuitively or calculatedly, that their self-absorbed posturing will strike a chord among their peers.

But Denver was never a teenybopper, never a droning adolescent. He dealt in pure spring water, soaring eagles, summer rain – in a thigh-slapping, celebratory but adult interpretation of pantheism. And yet the fans continue to pay their carbon-copy tributes. 'With each new recording of John's, my life grew with him and his music. I became an environmentalist, and continued to enjoy the beautiful creation that God has given us to explore, love and protect.' This adherent gets close to idolatry: 'I thank him for allowing himself to be the instrument and voice of our love, our space, our spirit and our Creator.' One finds oneself able to respect such passion and yet feel mildly queasy. As Bob Dylan warned, no doubt for heartfelt reasons, 'Don't follow leaders.'

Another fan gives a possible clue to this worship. 'I reluctantly turned into an adult,' he says. 'Your music once again became an integral part of my life. As an avid backpacker/mountaineer, I have developed a keen awareness, love, and respect for nature.' This is strange – most of us cannot wait to turn into an adult. Of course, in maturer years we may sometimes yearn for what seemed to be the simpler pleasures and securities of youth, once a guaranteed warm bed and home cooking have been replaced by the worries of employment and the mortgage. But surely most of us did not move reluctantly into adulthood – we embraced it with fumbling but heady excitement.

An older admirer says: 'The maturity that John and I both [*sic*] have in common colours our lives, songs and the adventures that will come . . . Music mellows and relaxes with age, but our fervour about our lives and worlds becomes more intense. I guess it comes with a realisation of what really matters to us.' This tribute comes after the writer has detailed a lengthy series of coincidental parallels between events in her life and in Denver's, binding her to him.

Another fan attests to their ability to match all the important developments in their life to the Denver music current at the time, and gives a further clue to the performer's appeal. 'It is like listening to a friend singing in your living-room when you are at a concert with several thousand people.' As we have already noted this was undoubtedly a quality – a professional skill perhaps intuitively learned – central to Denver's appeal as a performer. It is noticeable how often professional critics who were basically unsympathetic to his music were forced to acknowledge his ability thus to 'work a room', even when that room was a huge auditorium.

Yet another writer goes further, referring to Denver as a friend, though it soon becomes clear that they have never met. 'It was a cold December day in an army base in Germany in 1972, when John and I became friends. It's a friendship that has helped me through the high and low points of my life.' So far, so real. It is then that unreality takes over. 'He never complained when I packed him away in boxes as we travelled the world and then pulled him out to show him off to my friends.' It is a nice and heartfelt image, though unfortunately it makes the great man sound like a glove puppet. This proprietorial attitude is not untypical of the effect Denver has, and of the power he wields. 'He is mine,' his fans seem to say, 'and I will always be very grateful for my unique relationship with him.'

A different relationship is that with Denver the healer of a bruised nation. 'With the end of the Vietnam War and the Watergate/Nixon fiasco fresh in our minds, we longed for something positive to uplift our shattered idealism. John was there – his music, his love of life, his message of hope, and of concern for others and the planet on which we dwell.' Few performers have exerted this kind of power, this spiritual balm. Stars as disparate as Elvis Presley and Barry Manilow have produced blind, uncritical quivering of the knees and all parts north, but nothing quite like this platonic sense of kinship. It is interesting, incidentally, that the last-quoted witness felt that the ignominious end to the war and the dodgy dealings at the Watergate building had 'shattered idealism', as if up until that point the war had been a glorious crusade and Nixon a decent sort of chap.

In another moving testimony the victim of a serious road accident says that, in the wake of newly-acquired and grievous physical and mental disabilities, they are now able to 'feel' Denver's songs. 'They mean so much to me now in such a different way and I am happy and grateful about that.'

I admit I get uneasy when Denver's fans begin to sound like right-wing fundamentalists, intentionally or not, sounding off about all that is impure in this world and comparing it to the bracing bleach of his music. 'When I listen to some of the lyrics of the heavy-metal groups and their suggestive phrases I wonder what is happening to the youth that listens to that type of garbage.' This could have been said by one of those ranting television evangelists on American cable stations, the blue-chinned, ochre-tanned, white-supremacy kind who ask the gullible to send them lots of dollars to assist in the Lord's work. Presumably the 'suggestive phrases' refer to the sex act, the process whereby we all arrived on Earth, and the topic of most interest to most young people.

However, whatever reservations an objective observer of Denver's extraordinary power as a performer may have about the devotion he inspires, no one could fail to be struck by its sincerity and, one suspects, its power for good.

John Denver was cremated on Wednesday, 15 October and his ashes were carried home to Aspen on the following day by his friend Jerry Jampolsky. On the Friday at 10 a.m. a service was held at the church that his mother attended, the Faith Presbyterian in Aurora. His brother, Ron Deutschendorf, had

170

assembled a playlist of songs to cover the period during which the mourners entered the church, and for the service itself.

They were 'Poems, Prayers and Promises', The Beatles's 'Let It Be', 'My Sweet Lady', 'Wooden Indian', Paul McCartney's 'Junk', 'Gospel Changes', 'Take Me Home, Country Roads', 'I Guess He'd Rather Be in Colorado', 'Sunshine on My Shoulders', 'Around and Around', 'Fire and Rain' and, during the service, 'On the Wings of a Dream', 'High Flight', 'Perhaps Love' and 'The Wings that Fly Us Home'.

On the Saturday there was an opportunity for a greater number – around 1,200 – to share their grief at a further memorial event. This was held in Aspen at the open-air amphitheatre known as the Music Tent, under a crisp, blue autumn sky with the backdrop of the sunlit mountains. The *Rocky Mountain News* quoted Denver's close friend and Windstar partner, Tom Crum: 'We suspect that John is here. We know he is in the mountains and the streams.' This, of course, is a neat summary, one might say an exemplary definition, of pantheistic belief. Another example of this spiritual sensation springs to mind – when the great British blues singer Jo Ann Kelly was dying, cruelly young, of a brain tumour, she told her friends to listen out for the wind rattling around their windows in future, because it would mean that she was there.

Denver's two ex-wives, Annie and Cassandra, were united in mourning and, in spite of their tempestuous divorces, both paid warm tribute. 'Bottom line is, he was always here for me,' said Annie, 'and now he isn't. This is all for you, John, and I hope you're really at peace and in God's grace.' Cassandra added: 'Pain by itself is merely pain, but pain coupled with suffering is meaningful. Suffering can endure because there is a reason that is worth the effort. I can't begin to tell you how grateful I am that most recently John and I learned about forgiveness.'

Of course all bereavement leaves an uncompleted relationship behind it, but this hint that Denver and Cassie were overcoming

171

the bitterness of the past, even moving towards reconciliation, was particularly poignant.

Lyle Lovett paid his own tribute to a man he called a hero, and sang 'Texas River Song'. Angling pal Red Dodge recalled Denver's typical fisherman's lies, while Bill Twist talked about their last round of golf. While his companions decided to play a second round in the afternoon, Denver left to try out his plane – with a promise to meet up again for dinner. The meal continued without him, though his friends were still unaware of the reason for his absence. As they walked through Monterey afterwards they found a golf ball in the street. Symbolically, it was Twist's favoured brand, the Titleist 3 Professional 100, and over the years Denver had spent any amount of time helping Twist search for lost balls in the rough. 'I don't know how it works,' said Twist at the memorial event, 'but I know that golf ball was a gift and it's one I'll never lose.'

During his career, in spite of success that broke all records, Denver had never been given a Grammy award to mark any of his achievements. After his death belated amends were made, admittedly some way down the honours board, when his last album *All Aboard* was given the 1997 prize as 'Best Musical Album for Children'. At the Radio City Music Hall in New York, scene of the awards dinner, Jesse Belle received the trophy, modelled on an old-fashioned gramophone with a trumpet-shaped speaker.

Another posthumous award came in the form of an honorary PhD degree in Humanities, given to him by the Daystar Commission in Des Moines, Iowa. The citation referred to his 'significant, original, personally designed and carried out musical, literary, environmental and humanitarian work'.

The Birchmere Music Hall in Alexandria, Virginia, was the venue for a Denver tribute concert on 16 January 1998, organised under the auspices of the World Folk Music Association. Although the hall holds only 500 people and could probably have been filled several times over, given the impressive bill of Denver's colleagues and musical friends who assembled for the evening, the small scale did guarantee an appropriate intimacy. There was a deliberate attempt to recapture the spirit of the old Cellar Door days.

Two members of Denver's last band, guitarist Pete Huttlinger and keyboard player Chris Nole, contributed instrumental versions of such favourites as 'The Eagle and the Hawk', 'Poems, Prayers and Promises' and 'For You', and finished with 'Eagles and Horses'. A version of 'That's the Way It's Gonna Be' by Doris Justis and Sean McGhee, with Paul Prestopino on guitar, revived Cellar Door memories of the Chad Mitchell Trio. Emma Danoff, daughter of Fat City's Bill Danoff and Taffy Neivert, sang 'Leaving on a Jet Plane', and then it was Tom Paxton's turn.

Together with Dick Kniss and Pete Kennedy, Paxton performed 'Forest Lawns', 'Whose Garden Was This?' and 'Jimmy Newman'. Donal Lease, who would have been a potential new recruit to Denver's band, sang 'Sunshine', 'For You' and Pete Seeger's 'Bells of Rhymney', and recalled the time that Denver had visited his apartment above the Cellar Door eager to play a new album he'd just bought – *Sgt Pepper's Lonely Hearts Club Band.* Other contributors to a warmly received first half included Steve Weisberg, Jon Carroll, Margot Kunkel and Mack Bailey, while Bill and Taffy sang their archetypal Denver song 'I Guess He'd Rather Be in Colorado'.

After the interval, various permutations of Fat City and the Starland Vocal Band performed, and Paxton read out a letter from Milt Okun, who pointed out that the longevity of the songs, and their acceptance into America's cultural mainstream, was an eloquent answer to Denver's critics. Kris O'Connor accepted a posthumous Lifetime Achievement award from the WFMA on behalf of Denver before the songs continued, ending with 'Take Me Home, Country Roads'. In bringing together musicians whose lives had chimed with Denver's throughout his career, in an affectionate spirit of tribute, the evening was deemed a huge nostalgic success.

Later in the year came the news that the National Arbor Day Foundation had granted $10,000 to Aspen towards planting a grove of trees in Denver's memory, dedicated in a late-summer ceremony. According to the *Aspen Times* the initial approach to the Foundation had come from the World Family of John Denver, formed to keep his campaigning spirit alive. The scheme coincided with the local council's wish to replant the banks of the Roaring Fork river flowing through Aspen. Tree-planting was considered a more suitable tribute than, say, renaming Aspen's Main Street after Denver.

In the meantime, a further local recognition of Denver's celebrity had already taken place. The Aspen Skiing Company had designated 22 March 1998 as John Denver Day, and had named their highest ski run – the highest lift-served ski run in the country, indeed – as Rocky Mountain High. Appropriately, it was also announced that the lift taking skiers up to this run in Snowmass was now totally wind-powered, in that it was driven by electricity generated solely from wind turbines. The company running the ski centre made a donation to the Windstar Land Conservancy, and unveiled a 'Rocky Mountain High' plaque in Denver's honour, which is inscribed with a verse of 'The Eagle and the Hawk'.

When a pop singer dies he usually leaves us only with his music. Denver's lifetime of ecological activism has left an example behind as well, and numerous practical and positive legacies. Although he became involved in any number of causes, they were united in their attempts to improve our relationship with the planet. It is this relationship that was at the heart of Denver's finest work.

Discography

This discography lists in order the main sequence of John Denver's releases on RCA and Windstar during his life, together with a selection of the many compilations available over the years.

RHYMES AND REASONS (OCTOBER 1969)

The Love of the Common People/ Catch Another Butterfly/ Daydream/ The Ballad of Spiro Agnew/ Circus/ When I'm Sixty-Four/ The Ballad of Richard Nixon/ Rhymes and Reasons/ Yellow Cat/ Leaving on a Jet Plane/ (You Dun Stomped) On My Heart/ My Old Man/ I Wish I Knew How It Would Feel to Be Free/ Today Is the First Day of the Rest of My Life

TAKE ME TO TOMORROW (MAY 1970)

Take Me to Tomorrow/ Isabel/ Follow Me/ Forest Lawn/ Aspenglow/ Amsterdam/ Anthem Revelation/ Sticky Summer Weather/ Carolina in My Mind/ Jimmy Newman/ Molly

WHOSE GARDEN WAS THIS? (OCTOBER 1970)

Tremble If You Must/ Sail Away Home/ The Night They Drove Old Dixie Down/ Mr Bojangles/ I Wish I Could Have Been There/ Whose Garden Was This?/ The Game is Over/ Eleanor Rigby/ Old Folks/ Medley: Golden Septembers, Sweet Sweet Life, Tremble If You Must/ Jingle Bells

POEMS, PRAYERS AND PROMISES (MAY 1971)

Poems, Prayers and Promises/ Let It Be/ My Sweet Lady/ Wooden Indian/ Junk/ Gospel Changes/ Take Me Home, Country Roads/ I Guess He'd Rather Be in Colorado/ Sunshine on My Shoulders/ Around and Around/ Fire and Rain/ The Box

AERIE (FEBRUARY 1972)

Starwood in Aspen/ Everyday/ Casey's Last Ride/ City of New Orleans/ Friends with You/ 60-second Song for a Bank – 'May We Help You Today?'/ Blow up Your TV/ All of My Memories/ She Won't Let Me Fly Away/ Readjustment Blues/ The Eagle and the Hawk/ Tools

ROCKY MOUNTAIN HIGH (SEPTEMBER 1972)

Rocky Mountain High/ Mother Nature's Son/ Paradise/ For Baby (For Bobbie)/ Darcy Farrow/ Prisoners/ Goodbye Again/ Season Suite: Summer, Fall, Winter, Late Winter, Early Spring, Spring

FAREWELL ANDROMEDA (JUNE 1973)

I'd Rather Be a Cowboy/ Berkeley Woman/ Please, Daddy (Don't Get Drunk This Christmas)/ Angel from Montgomery/ River of Love/ Rocky Mountain Suite (Cold Nights in Canada)/ Whiskey Basin Blues/ Sweet Misery/ Zachary and Jennifer/ We Don't Live Here No More/ Farewell Andromeda (Welcome to My Morning)

JOHN DENVER'S GREATEST HITS (NOVEMBER 1973)

Take Me Home, Country Roads/ Follow Me/ Starwood in Aspen/ For Baby (For Bobbie)/ Rhymes and Reasons/ Leaving on a Jet Plane/ The Eagle and the Hawk/ Sunshine on My Shoulders/ Goodbye Again/ Poems, Prayers and Promises/ Rocky Mountain High

BACK HOME AGAIN (MARCH 1974)

Back Home Again/ On the Road/ Grandma's Feather Bed/ Matthew/ Thank God I'm a Country Boy/ The Music Is You/ Annie's Song/ It's up to You/ Cool an' Green an' Shady/ Eclipse/ Sweet Surrender/ This Old Guitar

AN EVENING WITH JOHN DENVER (FEBRUARY 1975)

The Music Is You/ Farewell Andromeda (Welcome to My Morning)/ Mother Nature's Son/ Summer/ Today/ Saturday Night in Toledo, Ohio/ Matthew/ Rocky Mountain Suite (Cold Nights in Canada)/ Sweet Surrender/ Grandma's Feather Bed/ Annie's Song/ The Eagle and the Hawk/ My Sweet Lady/ Annie's Other Song/ Boy from the Country/ Rhymes and Reasons/ Forest Lawn/ Pickin' the Sun Down/ Thank God I'm a Country Boy/ Take Me Home, Country Roads/

Poems, Prayers and Promises/ Rocky Mountain High/ This Old Guitar

WINDSONG (SEPTEMBER 1975)

Windsong/ Cowboy's Delight/ Spirit/ Looking for Space/ Shipmates and Cheyenne/ Late Nite Radio/ Love Is Everywhere/ Two Shots/ I'm Sorry/ Fly Away/ Calypso/ Song of Wyoming

ROCKY MOUNTAIN CHRISTMAS (NOVEMBER 1975)

Aspenglow/ The Christmas Song (Chestnuts Roasting on an Open Fire)/ Rudolf the Red-Nosed Reindeer/ Silver Bells/ Please, Daddy (Don't Get Drunk This Christmas)/ Christmas for Cowboys/ Away in a Manger/ What Child Is This?/ Coventry Carol/ Oh Holy Night/ Silent Night, Holy Night/ A Baby Just Like You

LIVE IN LONDON (1976)

Amsterdam/ Annie's Song/ Back Home Again/ Calypso/ Grandma's Feather Bed/ Leaving on a Jet Plane/ Pickin' the Sun Down/ Spirit/ Starwood in Aspen/ Sunshine on My Shoulders/ Take Me Home, Country Roads/ Thank God I'm a Country Boy/ The Eagle and the Hawk

SPIRIT (AUGUST 1976)

Come and Let Me Look in Your Eyes/ Eli's Song/ Wrangell Mountain Song/ Hitchhiker/ In a Grand Way/ Polka Dots and Moonbeams/ It Makes Me Giggle/ Baby, You Look Good to Me Tonight/ Like a Sad

Song/ San Antonio Rose/ Pegasus/ The Wings that Fly Us Home

JOHN DENVER'S GREATEST HITS, VOLUME 2 (MARCH 1977)

Annie's Song/ Farewell Andromeda (Welcome to My Morning)/ Fly Away/ Like a Sad Song/ Looking for Space/ Thank God I'm a Country Boy/ Grandma's Feather Bed/ Back Home Again/ I'm Sorry/ My Sweet Lady/ Calypso/ This Old Guitar

I WANT TO LIVE (NOVEMBER 1977)

How Can I Leave You Again/ Tradewinds/ Bet on the Blues/ It Amazes Me/ To the Wild Country/ Ripplin' Waters/ Thirsty Boots/ Dearest Esmerelda/ Singing Skies and Dancing Waters/ I Want to Live/ Druthers

JOHN DENVER (JANUARY 1978)

Downhill Stuff/ Sweet Melinda/ What's on Your Mind/ Joseph and Joe/ Life Is So Good/ Berkeley Woman/ Johnny B. Goode/ You're So Beautiful/ Southwind/ Garden Song/ Songs of . . .

LIVE AT THE SYDNEY OPERA HOUSE (1978)

Rocky Mountain High/ Back Home Again/ Fly Away/ Looking for Space/ I Want to Live/ It's a Sin to Tell a Lie/ Moreton Bay/ Grandma's Feather Bed/ Thank God I'm a Country Boy/ Take Me Home, Country Roads/ The Eagle and the Hawk/ Annie's Song

A CHRISTMAS TOGETHER (OCTOBER 1979)

Twelve Days of Christmas/ Have Yourself a Merry Little Christmas/ The Peace Carol/ Christmas is Coming/ A Baby Just Like You/ Deck the Halls/ When the River Meets the Sea/ Little Saint Nick/ Noel, Christmas Eve 1913/ The Christmas Wish/ Medley: Alfie the Christmas Tree, Carol for a Christmas Tree, It's in Every One of Us/ Silent Night, Holy Night/ We Wish You a Merry Christmas

AUTOGRAPH (FEBRUARY 1980)

Dancing with the Mountains/ The Mountain Song/ How Mountain Girls Can Love/ Song for the Life/ The Ballad of St Anne's Reel/ In My Heart/ Wrangell Mountain Song/ Whalebones and Crosses/ American Child/ You Say that the Battle Is Over/ Autograph

SOME DAYS ARE DIAMONDS (JUNE 1981)

Some Days Are Diamonds (Some Days Are Stones)/ Gravel on the Ground/ San Francisco Mabel Joy/ Sleepin' Alone/ Easy on Easy Street/ The Cowboy and the Lady/ Country Love/ Till You Opened My Eyes/ Wild Flowers in a Mason Jar/ Boy from the Country

SEASONS OF THE HEART (FEBRUARY 1982)

Seasons of the Heart/ Opposite Tables/ Relatively Speaking/ Dreams/ Nothing but a Breeze/ What One Man Can Do/ Shanghai Breezes/ Islands/ Heart to Heart/ Perhaps Love/ Children of the Universe

IT'S ABOUT TIME (SEPTEMBER 1983)

Hold on Tightly/ Thought of You/ Somethin' About/ On the Wings of a Dream/ Flight/ Falling out of Love/ I Remember Romance/ Wild Montana Skies/ World Game/ It's About Time

ROCKY MOUNTAIN HOLIDAY (NOVEMBER 1983)

Hey Old Pal/ Grandma's Feather Bed/ She'll Be Comin' Round the Mountain/ Catch Another Butterfly/ Down by the Old Mill Stream/ Durango Mountain Caballero/ Gone Fishin'/ Medley: Tumbling Tumbleweeds, Happy Trails/ Poems, Prayers and Promises/ Take 'em Away/ Going Camping/ Home on the Range/ No One Like You

JOHN DENVER'S GREATEST HITS, VOLUME 3 (NOVEMBER 1984)

How Can I Leave You Again/ Some Days Are Diamonds (Some Days Are Stones)/ Shanghai Breezes/ Seasons of the Heart/ Perhaps Love/ Love Again/ Dancing with the Mountains/ Wild Montana Skies/ I Want to Live/ The Gold and Beyond/ Autograph

DREAMLAND EXPRESS (JUNE 1985)

Dreamland Express/ Claudette/ Gimme Your Love/ Got My Heart Set on You/ If Ever/ The Harder They Fall/ Don't Close Your Eyes Tonight/ A Wild Heart Looking for Home/ I'm in the Mood to Be Desired/ Trail of Tears/ African Sunrise

One World (June 1986)

Love is the Master/ Love Again/ I Remember You/ Hey There, Mr Lonely Heart/ Let Us Begin/ Along for the Ride ('56 T-Bird)/ I Can't Escape/ True Love Takes Time/ One World/ It's a Possibility/ Flying for Me

Higher Ground (September 1989)

Higher Ground/ Homegrown Tomatoes/ Whispering Jesse/ Never a Doubt/ Deal with the Ladies/ Sing Australia/ A Country Girl in Paris/ For You/ All This Joy/ Falling Leaves (The Refugees)/ Bread and Roses/ Alaska and Me

Christmas, Like a Lullaby (November 1989)

Christmas, Like a Lullaby/ The First Noel/ Away in a Manger/ The Children of Bethlehem/ Jingle Bells/ White Christmas/ Marvellous Toy/ Blue Christmas/ Rudolph the Red-Nosed Reindeer/ Little Drummer Boy/ Mary's Little Boy Child/ The Christmas Song (Chestnuts Roasting on an Open Fire)/ Have Yourself a Merry Little Christmas

Earth Songs (February 1990)

Windsong/ Rocky Mountain Suite (Cold Nights in Canada)/ Rocky Mountain High/ Sunshine on My Shoulders/ The Eagle and the Hawk/ Eclipse/ The Flower that Shattered the Stone/ Raven's Child/ Children of the Universe/ To the Wild Country/ American Child/ Calypso/ Islands/ Earth Day Every Day (Celebrate)

THE FLOWER THAT SHATTERED THE STONE (SEPTEMBER 1990)

The Flower that Shattered the Stone/ Thanks to You/ Postcard from Paris/ High, Wide and Handsome/ Eagles and Horses/ A Little Further North/ Raven's Child/ Ancient Rhymes/ The Gift You Are/ I Watch You Sleeping/ Stonehaven Sunset/ The Flower that Shattered the Stone (Reprise)

DIFFERENT DIRECTIONS (SEPTEMBER 1991)

Potter's Wheel/ Ponies/ The Foxfire Suite: Spring is Alive, You Are . . ., Whisper the Wind, Spring is Alive (Reprise)/ Chained to the Wheel/ Two Different Directions/ Hold on to Me/ The Chosen Ones/ Amazon (Let This Be a Voice)/ Tenderly Calling

THE WILDLIFE CONCERT (1995: ALSO RELEASED AS A VIDEO)

Rocky Mountain High/ Rhymes and Reasons/ Take Me Home, Country Roads/ Back Home Again/ I Guess He'd Rather Be in Colorado/ Matthew/ Sunshine on My Shoulders/ You Say the Battle Is Over/ Eagles and Horses/ Darcy Farrow/ Whispering Jesse/ Me and My Uncle/ Wild Montana Skies/ Medley: Leaving on a Jet Plane, Goodbye Again/ Bet on the Blues/ The Harder They Fall/ Shanghai Breezes/ Fly Away/ A Song for All Lovers/ Dreamland Express/ For You/ Is It Love?/ Falling out of Love/ Annie's Song/ Poems, Prayers and Promises/ Calypso/ Amazon/ This Old Guitar

THE UNPLUGGED COLLECTION (1996)

Annie's Song/ Perhaps Love/ Dreamland Express/ Rocky Mountain High/ Seasons of the Heart/ Whispering Jesse/ Take Me Home, Country Roads/ For You/ Windsong/ Leaving on a Jet Plane/ I'm Sorry/ Back Home Again/ Sunshine on My Shoulders/ Thank God I'm a Country Boy/ Christmas for Cowboys/ Love Again

ALL ABOARD (1997)

Jenny Dreamed of Trains/ Freight Train Boogie/ Steel Rails/ Waiting for a Train/ Been Working on the Railroad/ On the Atchison/ Old Train/ Daddy, What's a Train/ The Little Engine that Could/ Last Train Gone Down/ Last Hobo/ People Get Ready/ Lining Track/ City of New Orleans/ Song for Jesse Belle

COLLECTIONS

The John Denver repertoire has been constantly recycled, and sometimes different anthologies have appeared in different territories. The following are some of the most notable compilations.

THE COUNTRY ROADS COLLECTION

Leaving on a Jet Plane/ Circus/ Rhymes and Reasons/ Catch Another Butterfly/ Daydream/ Follow Me/ Aspenglow/ Molly/ Sticky Summer Weather/ Isabel/ Sunshine on My Shoulders/ My Sweet Lady/ Take Me Home, Country Roads/ I Guess He'd Rather Be in Colorado/ Poems, Prayers and Promises/ Starwood in Aspen/ City of New Orleans/ All of My Memories/ Casey's Last Ride/ The Eagle and the Hawk/ Friends with You/ Rocky Mountain High/ For Baby (For

Bobbie)/ Goodbye Again/ We Don't Live Here No More/ I'd Rather Be a Cowboy (Lady's Chains)/ Farewell Andromeda (Welcome to My Morning)/ Rocky Mountain Suite (Cold Nights in Canada)/ Annie's Song/ Back Home Again/ Grandma's Feather Bed/ Sweet Surrender/ Eclipse/ Thank God I'm a Country Boy/ This Old Guitar/ Spirit/ Song of Wyoming/ I'm Sorry/ Windsong/ Looking for Space/ Fly Away/ Calypso/ Come and Let Me Look in Your Eyes/ Like a Sad Song/ Polka Dots and Moonbeams/ In the Grand Way/ How Can I Leave You Again/ Ripplin' Waters/ It Amazes Me/ Singing Skies and Dancing Waters/ Dearest Esmerelda/ Thirsty Boots/ I Want to Live/ Southwind/ Garden Song/ What's on Your Mind/ You're So Beautiful/ In My Heart/ The Mountain Song/ Song for the Life/ Autograph/ Some Days are Diamonds (Some Days are Stone)/ Country Love/ Dreams/ Heart to Heart/ Shanghai Breezes/ Seasons of the Heart/ Perhaps Love (with Placido Domingo) */ Falling out of Love/ It's About Time/ Wild Montana Skies* (with Emmylou Harris) */ Dreamland Express/ If Ever/ I'm in the Mood to be Desired Tonight/ Don't Close your Eyes Tonight/ Love is the Master/ I Can't Escape/ Love Again/ Flying for Me*

THE ROCKY MOUNTAIN COLLECTION

Leaving on a Jet Plane/ Rhymes and Reasons/ Follow Me/ Aspenglow/ Sunshine on My Shoulders/ My Sweet Lady/ Take Me Home, Country Roads/ Poems, Prayers and Promises/ The Eagle and the Hawk/ Starwood in Aspen/ Friends with You/ Goodbye Again/ Rocky Mountain High/ I'd Rather Be a Cowboy (Lady's Chains)/ Farewell Andromeda (Welcome to My Morning)/ Back Home Again/ Annie's Song/ Thank God I'm a Country Boy/ Sweet Surrender/ This Old Guitar/ Fly Away/ Looking for Space/ Windsong/ Calypso/ I'm Sorry/ Like a Sad Song/ Come and Let Me Look in Your Eyes/ How Can I Leave You Again/ Thirsty Boots/ It Amazes Me/ I Want to Live/ Autograph/ Some Days are Diamonds (Some Days are Stone)/

Seasons of the Heart/ Shanghai Breezes/ Perhaps Love (with Placido Domingo) / *Wild Montana Skies* (with Emmylou Harris) / *Love Again/ Flying for Me*

REFLECTIONS: SONGS OF LOVE AND LIFE

You're So Beautiful/ Dearest Esmerelda/ Annie's Song/ My Sweet Lady/ Polka Dots and Moonbeams/ For Baby (For Bobbie)/ Come and Let Me Look in Your Eyes/ Daydream/ Let It Be/ What's on Your Mind/ I'm Sorry/ Rhymes and Reasons/ Molly/ Sunshine on My Shoulders/ How Can I Leave You Again/ Fire and Rain/ Isabel/ Goodbye Again/ Autograph/ Calypso

THE JOHN DENVER COLLECTION

Take Me Home, Country Roads/ Homegrown Tomatoes/ Eagles and Horses/ Ponie/ High Wide and Handsome/ Hold on to Me/ Whispering Jessie/ Never a Doubt/ The Eagle and the Hawk/ For You/ Windsong/ Annie's Song/ Potter's Wheel/ Two Different Directions/ Chained to the Wheel/ A Country Girl in Paris/ All This Joy/ Thanks to You/ The Gift You Are/ I Want to Live/ Rocky Mountain High/ To the Wild Country/ The Chosen Ones/ The Foxfire Suite/ Higher Ground/ Raven's Child/ Bread and Roses/ Rocky Mountain Suite/ Grandma's Feather Bed/ The Marvellous Toy/ Sunshine on My Shoulders/ Deal with the Ladies/ Amazon/ Eclipse/ Earth Day Every Day (Celebrate)/ Ancient Rhymes/ Tenderly Calling/ Falling Leaves (Refugees)/ Islands/ Children of the Universe/ Calypso/ The Flower that Shattered the Stone/ American Child/ Postcard from Paris/ In a Far Away Land/ A Little Further North/ Sing Australia/ Alaska and Me/ Stonehaven Sunset/ Potter's Wheel (Live)/ The Flower that Shattered the Stone (Reprise)

Acknowledgements

I wish to offer my grateful thanks to Mark Rhodes, the Strategic Marketing Manager of BMG Australia Limited, who not only represents John Denver in that part of the world on behalf of RCA, but who was also a good friend of the singer. Mark took an interest in this project from the start, and was very helpful via faxes, telephone calls and mail. In addition, he kindly gave up some time to talk to me during a busy trip to the UK late in 1998. I have not quoted Mark directly, but found his enthusiasm and knowledge invaluable in building up a picture of Denver.

Bibliography

The following were used freely, and with gratitude. Wherever possible they have been directly credited in the text as well as here.

Take Me Home: An Autobiography by John Denver with Arthur Tobier (Headline, 1994)

Alaska: a Challenge for Democracy by John Denver

Free Spirit: the World Family of John Denver, various

Billboard, various

Rolling Stone, various

Melody Maker, various

Obituaries and news stories on Denver's death published in *The Times, The Independent, Rolling Stone, Country Music Round-up, The Guardian, Daily Mail, North Country, Country Music News & Routes, Country Music People, Daily Telegraph, The Express, Daily Mirror*

'Things to do in Denver . . .', *The Guardian* (29 August 1998)

'Third of all nature lost in 25 years', *The Independent* (2 October 1998)

'Eco-terrorists burn ski resort', *The Independent* (23 October 1998)

'Exxon Valdez study shows new oil menace', *The Observer* (7 March 1999)

'Exxon challenges payout a decade after Valdez spill', *The Times* (date unknown)

'John Denver Memories', 'More JD Memories', Internet pages

'John Denver Remembered by the Old Cellar Door Gang' by Mary Ledford (source and date unknown)

'John Denver Online' (2 August 1995)

'John Denver: the Sunshine Boy', *Newsweek* (20 December 1976)

'This Country Boy Has Struck It Rich' by Peter J. Oppenheimer, *Family Weekly* (22 May 1977)

'Denver's Sweetness Suits His Fans' by Laura Fissinger, *St Paul Dispatch* (17 June 1982)

'John Denver: So Square that He's Hip?' by Lou Carlozo, *Chicago Tribune* (6 March 1996)

'Crowd-Pleasing Denver Delivers Richer Versions of Beautiful Oldies' by Miriam Di Nunzio, *Chicago Sun Times* (10 March 1996)

'Road to Hell', *FHM* (June 1997)

John Denver: A Portrait (Windstar Video, 1994)